CLASSIC COOKING FOR
CHRISTMAS

CLASSIC COOKING FOR
CHRISTMAS

A SEASONAL COLLECTION OF OVER 100 FESTIVE RECIPES
SHOWN IN MORE THAN 450 TEMPTING PHOTOGRAPHS

MARTHA DAY

southwater

This edition is published by Southwater, an imprint of
Anness Publishing Ltd, Hermes House, 88–89 Blackfriars Road,
London SE1 8HA;
tel. 020 7401 2077; fax 020 7633 9499

www.southwaterbooks.com; www.annesspublishing.com

If you like the images in this book and would like to investigate
using them for publishing, promotions or advertising, please visit our
website www.practicalpictures.com for more information.

UK distributor: Book Trade Services; tel. 0116 2759086;
fax 0116 2759090; uksales@booktradeservices.com;
exportsales@booktradeservices.com
North American agent/distributor: National Book Network;
tel. 301 459 3366; fax 301 429 5746; www.nbnbooks.com
Australian agent/distributor: Pan Macmillan Australia; tel. 1300 135 113;
fax 1300 135 103; customer.service@macmillan.com.au
New Zealand agent/distributor: David Bateman Ltd;
tel. (09) 415 7664; fax (09) 415 8892

Publisher: Joanna Lorenz
Editor: Anne Hildyard
Photography: Karl Adamson, Steve Baxter, James Duncan,
Michelle Garrett, Amanda Heywood,
Don Last, Patrick McLeavey
Recipes: Carla Capalbo, Jacqueline Clark, Carole Clements,
Roz Denny, Nicola Diggins, Joanna Farrow, Christine France,
Silvana Franco, Christine Ingram, Judy Jackson, Elizabeth Lambert
Oritz, Wendy Lee, Jane Stevenson, Laura Washburn,
Pamela Westland, Steven Wheeler, Elizabeth Wolf-Cohen
Jacket Design: Graham Webb
Proofreading Manager: Lindsay Zamponi
Production Controller: Christine Ni

© Anness Publishing Ltd 2010

ETHICAL TRADING POLICY

Because of our ongoing ecological investment programme,
you, as our customer, can have the pleasure and reassurance
of knowing that a tree is being cultivated on your behalf to
naturally replace the materials used to make the book you are
holding. For further information about this scheme, go to
www.annesspublishing.com/trees

NOTES

Bracketed terms are intended for American readers.
For all recipes, quantities are given in both metric and imperial
measures and, where appropriate, in standard cups and spoons.
Follow one set of measures, but not a mixture, because they are
not interchangeable.
Standard spoon and cup measures are level. 1 tsp = 5ml, 1 tbsp
= 15ml, 1 cup = 250ml/8fl oz.
Australian standard tablespoons are 20ml. Australian readers
should use 3 tsp in place of 1 tbsp for measuring small quantities.
American pints are 16fl oz/2 cups. American readers should use
20fl oz/2.5 cups in place of 1 pint when measuring liquids.
Electric oven temperatures in this book are for conventional
ovens. When using a fan oven, the temperature will probably
need to be reduced by about 10–20°C/20–40°F. Since ovens
vary, you should check with your manufacturer's instruction book
for guidance. The nutritional analysis given for each recipe is
calculated per portion (i.e. serving or item), unless otherwise
stated. If the recipe gives a range, such as Serves 4–6, then the
nutritional analysis will be for the smaller portion size, i.e. 6
servings. Measurements for sodium do not include salt added to
taste. Medium (US large) eggs are used unless otherwise stated.

PUBLISHER'S NOTE

Although the advice and information in this book are believed to be
accurate and true at the time of going to press, neither the authors
nor the publisher can accept any legal responsibility or liability for any
errors or omissions that may be made nor for any inaccuracies nor
for any loss, harm or injury that comes about from following
instructions or advice in this book.

Front cover shows Roast Turkey page 26. Previously published as
part of a larger volume, *The Ultimate Christmas Cookbook*

Contents

Introduction

Christmas is the time for high spirits and good cheer, a time for giving and for sharing. Food plays an essential part in the festive season: the gathering of friends and family around a table laden with rich and lavish fare goes hand-in-hand with our idea of what Christmas is all about.

While all cooks know the importance of good food at Christmas, they also know that great demands will be made on their time. The secret of a carefree Christmas lies in the planning. Thinking ahead and preparing in advance mean that decision-making under pressure is avoided. As the holidays get closer, the list of things to do gets longer: planning meals and menus, shopping for the freshest and choicest ingredients, followed by all the necessary roasting, chopping, kneading and baking. The excitement mounts as each task is crossed off the list. The preparation of Christmas foods is as much a part of Christmas as the eating and can be just as much fun if you include the whole family by delegating tasks.

This book is packed with inspirational recipes to take the cook smoothly through the festive season. There are more than 100 recipes to choose from, including all the traditional favourites, plus a range of tempting alternative dishes that are every bit as festive as the customary fare. Why not try this sample menu for your main meal: for Christmas dinner, start with Roquefort Tartlets, followed by Roast Turkey served with Festive Brussels Sprouts, Apricot and Raisin Stuffing and Cranberry Sauce. Finish with Traditional Christmas Pudding and Rum Butter. For vegetarians, you could serve Christmas Salad as an appetizer, followed by Filo Vegetable Pie served with Peas with Baby Onions and Cream, ending the feast with Crunchy Apple and Almond Flan. If you still can eat anything else, have some delicious bakes on hand to serve at teatime: try Festive Gingerbread or Almond Mincemeat Tartlets, and of course Moist and Rich Christmas Cake. All of the recipes in this book are tried and tested and shown in easy-to-follow photographic sequences to ensure success, and to guarantee that this Christmas is a happy and memorable one for everyone.

Right: Natural decorations are by far the most beautiful. Here, bundles of cinnamon sticks are tied together with ribbon and embellished with redcurrants for a scented tree trim.

Festive Starters

*C*hristmas is all about anticipation: the people you will
see, the gifts you will exchange and, of course, the Christmas
meals you'll eat together. A Christmas meal is like a good
novel – a tempting starter that builds to an exciting middle and
leads on to a satisfying ending. All of the festive starters in this
chapter will tempt the senses, and the trick is to make a good
match between the colours, textures and richness of all your
courses. Virtually any will complement the traditional turkey, but
keep in mind Pumpkin Soup for a beautiful colour contrast, or
Oriental Duck Consommé for an exotic touch. Farmhouse Pâté
will balance lighter fish or chicken lunches, while Grilled Brie
and Walnuts or Roquefort Tartlets will suit beef or lamb dishes.

CARROT AND CORIANDER SOUP

Nearly all root vegetables make excellent soups as they purée well and have an earthy flavour that

complements the sharper flavours of herbs and spices. Carrots are particularly versatile, and

this simple soup is elegant in both flavour and appearance.

INGREDIENTS

*450g/1lb carrots, preferably young
and tender
15ml/1 tbsp sunflower oil
40g/1½oz/3 tbsp butter
1 onion, chopped
1 celery stick, plus 2–3 pale leafy
celery tops
2 small potatoes, chopped
1 litre/1¾ pints/4 cups chicken stock
10–15ml/2–3 tsp ground coriander
15ml/1 tbsp chopped
fresh coriander (cilantro)
200ml/7fl oz/⅞ cup milk
salt and freshly ground
black pepper*

Serves 4–6

1 Trim the carrots and peel them if necessary, then cut into chunks. Heat the oil and 25g/1oz/2 tbsp of the butter in a large flameproof, casserole or heavy-based saucepan and fry the onion over a gentle heat for 3–4 minutes until slightly softened, but not browned.

2 Cut the celery stick into slices. Add the celery and potatoes to the onion in the pan, cook for a few minutes and then add the carrots. Fry over a gentle heat for 3–4 minutes, stirring, and then cover. Reduce the heat and sweat for 10 minutes. Shake the pan occasionally so that the vegetables do not stick.

3 Add the stock, bring to the boil and then partially cover and simmer for a further 8–10 minutes until the carrots and potatoes are tender.

4 Remove 6–8 tiny celery leaves for use as a garnish and finely chop the remaining celery tops (about 15ml/ 1 tbsp once chopped). Melt the remaining butter in a small saucepan and fry the ground coriander for about 1 minute, stirring constantly.

5 Reduce the heat and add the finely chopped celery and fresh coriander and fry over a gentle heat for about 1 minute. Set aside.

6 Process the soup in a food processor or blender until smooth and pour into a clean saucepan. Stir in the milk, coriander mixture and seasoning. Heat gently, taste and adjust the seasoning as necessary. Serve the soup garnished with the reserved celery leaves.

COOK'S TIP

For a more piquant flavour, add a little lemon juice to the soup just before serving.

CREAM OF MUSHROOM SOUP

A good mushroom soup makes the most of the subtle and sometimes rather elusive flavour of mushrooms.

Button mushrooms are used here for their pale colour; chestnut or, better still, field mushrooms give

a fuller flavour but will turn the soup a darker shade of brown.

INGREDIENTS

*275g/10oz/3¼ cups button
(white) mushrooms
15ml/1 tbsp sunflower oil
40g/1½oz/3 tbsp butter
1 small onion, finely chopped
15ml/1 tbsp plain (all-purpose) flour
450ml/¾ pint/1¾ cups vegetable stock
450ml/¾ pint/1¾ cups milk
pinch of dried basil
30–45ml/2–3 tbsp single (light)
cream (optional)
fresh basil leaves, to garnish
salt and freshly ground black pepper*

Serves 4

1 Separate the mushroom caps from the stalks. Slice the caps and chop the stalks, keeping the two piles separate.

2 Heat the sunflower oil and half the butter in a heavy-based saucepan and add the chopped onion, mushroom stalks and ½–¾ of the sliced mushroom caps. Fry for 1–2 minutes, stirring often, and then cover and sweat over a gentle heat for 6–7 minutes, stirring.

3 Stir in the flour and cook for about 1 minute. Gradually add the stock and milk to make a smooth, thin sauce. Add the basil, and season with salt and pepper. Bring to the boil and then simmer, partly covered, for 15 minutes.

4 Allow the soup to cool slightly and then pour into a food processor or blender and process until smooth. Melt the remaining butter in a heavy-based frying pan, and fry the remaining mushrooms over a gentle heat for 3–4 minutes until they are just tender.

5 Pour the soup into a large, clean saucepan and stir in the sliced mushrooms. Heat until very hot but not boiling and add salt and ground black pepper to taste. Add a little of the single cream, if using. Ladle the soup into 4 warmed bowls and serve the soup at once, sprinkled with the fresh basil leaves.

Pumpkin Soup

The sweet flavour of pumpkin is good in soups, teaming well with other more savoury

ingredients such as potatoes to make a warm and comforting dish.

Ingredients

15ml/1 tbsp sunflower oil
25g/1oz/2 tbsp butter
1 large onion, sliced
675g/1½lb pumpkin, cut into large chunks
450g/1lb potatoes, sliced
600ml/1 pint/2½ cups vegetable stock
good pinch of nutmeg
5ml/1 tsp chopped fresh tarragon
600ml/1 pint/2½ cups milk
about 5–10ml/1–2 tsp lemon juice
salt and freshly ground black pepper

Serves 4–6

1 Heat the sunflower oil and butter in a frying pan and fry the onion for 4–5 minutes until softened. Stir frequently.

2 Transfer the onions to a large heavy saucepan and add the pumpkin and potato. Stir well, then cover with the lid and cook gently over a low heat for about 10 minutes until the vegetables are almost tender. Stir the vegetables occasionally to prevent them from sticking to the pan.

3 Stir in the stock, nutmeg, tarragon and seasoning. Bring the liquid to the boil and then simmer for about 10 minutes until the vegetables are completely tender.

4 Allow the liquid to cool slightly away from the heat, then pour into a food processor or blender and process until smooth. Pour the soup back into a clean saucepan and add the milk. Heat gently and then taste, adding the lemon juice and extra seasoning if necessary. Serve piping hot with crusty brown bread rolls.

Cook's Tip

Pumpkins are readily available in supermarkets throughout the winter months. Other seasonal vegetables, such as squashes, can also be used to make tempting Christmas soups.

ORIENTAL DUCK CONSOMMÉ

Christmas need not be about just traditional European flavours. This soup is both light

and rich at the same time and has intriguing flavours of Southeast Asia.

INGREDIENTS

*1 duck carcass (raw or cooked), plus
2 legs or any giblets, trimmed of fat
1 large onion, unpeeled, with root
end trimmed
2 carrots, cut into 5cm/2in pieces
1 parsnip, cut into 5cm/2in pieces
1 leek, cut into 5cm/2in pieces
2–4 garlic cloves, crushed
2.5cm/1in piece fresh root ginger, peeled
and sliced
15ml/1 tbsp black peppercorns
4–6 thyme sprigs, or 5ml/1 tsp dried thyme
1 small bunch coriander (6–8 sprigs),
leaves and stems separated*

For the Garnish
*1 small carrot
1 small leek, halved lengthways
4–6 shiitake mushrooms, thinly sliced
soy sauce
2 spring onions, thinly sliced
watercress or shredded Chinese
leaves (Chinese cabbage)
freshly ground black pepper*

Serves 4

1 Put the duck carcass, with the legs or giblets, the onion, carrots, parsnip, leek and garlic in a large saucepan. Add the ginger, peppercorns, thyme and coriander stems, cover with water and bring to the boil. Skim off any foam on the surface.

2 Reduce the heat and simmer for 1½–2 hours, Strain through a muslin-lined sieve into a bowl; discard the bones and vegetables. Cool the stock and chill overnight. Skim off any fat and blot the surface with kitchen paper to remove any traces of fat.

3 For the garnish, cut the carrot and leek into 5cm/2in pieces and then lengthways in thin slices. Slice into thin julienne strips. Place in a saucepan with the mushrooms. Add the stock, some soy sauce and pepper.

4 Bring to the boil over a medium heat, skimming off any foam that rises to the surface. Adjust the seasoning.
Stir in the spring onions and watercress or Chinese leaves. Serve the consommé sprinkled with the coriander leaves.

Warm Prawn Salad with Spicy Marinade

Most of the ingredients for this salad can be prepared in advance, but wait until just before serving to cook

the prawns and bacon. Spoon them over the salad and serve with hot herb and garlic bread.

INGREDIENTS

225g/8oz/2 cups large, cooked,
shelled prawns (shrimp)
225g/8oz smoked streaky (fatty)
bacon, chopped
mixed lettuce leaves, washed and dried
30ml/2 tbsp snipped fresh chives

For the Lemon and Chilli Marinade
1 garlic clove, crushed
finely grated rind of 1 lemon
15ml/1 tbsp lemon juice
60ml/4 tbsp olive oil
1.5ml/1¼ tsp chilli paste, or a large pinch
dried ground chilli
15ml/1 tbsp light soy sauce
salt and freshly ground black pepper

Serves 8

1 In a glass bowl, mix the prawns with the garlic, lemon rind and juice, 45ml/3 tbsp oil, the chilli paste and soy sauce. Season with salt and pepper. Cover with clear film and leave to marinate for at least one hour.

2 Gently cook the bacon in the remaining oil until crisp. Drain well.

3 Tear the lettuce into bitesize pieces and arrange on plates.

4 Just before serving, put the prawns with their marinade into a frying pan, bring to the boil, add the bacon and cook for one minute. Spoon over the salad and sprinkle with snipped chives.

SMOKED SALMON SALAD

This recipe works equally well using smoked trout in place of salmon. The dressing can be made in

advance and stored in the refrigerator until you are ready to eat.

INGREDIENTS

4 thin slices white bread
oil, for frying
paprika, for dusting
mixed lettuce leaves
25g/1oz Parmesan cheese
225g/8oz smoked salmon, thinly sliced
1 lemon, cut into wedges

For the Vinaigrette Dressing
90ml/6 tbsp olive oil
30ml/2 tbsp red wine vinegar
1 garlic clove, crushed
5ml/1 tsp Dijon mustard
5ml/1 tsp clear honey
15ml/1 tbsp chopped fresh parsley
2.5ml/½ tsp fresh thyme
10ml/2 tsp capers, chopped
salt and freshly ground black pepper

Serves 8

1 First make the dressing. Put all the ingredients into a screw-top jar and shake the jar well. Season to taste.

2 With a small star-shaped cutter, stamp out shapes from the bread. Heat 2.5cm/1in oil in a shallow frying pan until the oil is almost smoking (test it with a cube of bread: it should sizzle on the surface and brown within 30 seconds). Fry the croûtons in batches until golden brown. Remove the croûtons and drain on kitchen paper. Dust with paprika and leave to cool.

3 Wash the lettuce, dry the leaves and tear them into small bitesize pieces. Wrap the leaves in a clean, damp tea towel and keep the lettuce in the refrigerator until ready to serve.

4 Slice the Parmesan cheese into wafer-thin flakes with a vegetable peeler. Put the flakes into a dish and cover with clear film.

5 Cut the salmon into 1cm/½in strips no more than 5cm/2in long.

6 Arrange the lettuce on individual plates, scatter over the Parmesan flakes and arrange the salmon strips on top. Shake the dressing vigorously again and spoon over the salad. Scatter over the croûtons and place a lemon wedge on the side of each plate.

Christmas Salad

This light and refreshing first course can be prepared ahead of time and assembled just

before serving. It is perfect to cleanse the palate before a rich main course.

INGREDIENTS

Mixed red and green lettuce leaves
2 sweet pink grapefruit
2 small avocados, peeled and cubed

For the Dressing
90ml/6 tbsp light olive oil
30ml/2 tbsp red wine vinegar
1 garlic clove, crushed
5ml/1 tsp Dijon mustard
salt and freshly ground black pepper

For the Caramelized Orange Peel
4 oranges
50g/2oz/4 tbsp caster (superfine) sugar
60ml/4 tbsp cold water

Serves 8

1 For the caramelized peel, using a vegetable peeler, remove the rind from the oranges in thin strips and reserve the fruit. Scrape away the white pith from the rind with a sharp knife, and cut the rind in fine shreds.

2 Heat the sugar and water in a small pan until the sugar has dissolved. Add the shreds of orange rind, increase the heat and boil steadily for 5 minutes, until the rind is tender. Using two forks, remove the orange rind from the syrup and spread it out on a wire rack to dry. (This can be done the day before.) Reserve the syrup.

3 Wash and dry the lettuce and tear the leaves into bitesize pieces. Wrap them in a damp tea towel and chill. Over a bowl, cut the oranges and grapefruit into segments, removing the pith.

4 Put the dressing ingredients into a screw-top jar and shake vigorously to emulsify the dressing. Add the reserved orange-flavoured syrup and adjust the seasoning to taste. Arrange the salad ingredients on individual plates with the avocados, spoon over the dressing and scatter on the caramelized peel.

Goat's Cheese Soufflé

Make sure everyone is seated before the soufflé comes out of the oven because it will begin to deflate almost

immediately. This recipe works equally well with strong blue cheeses such as Roquefort.

INGREDIENTS

25g/1oz/2 tbsp butter
25g/1oz/2 tbsp plain (all-purpose) flour
175ml/6fl oz/¾ cup milk
1 bay leaf
freshly grated nutmeg
grated Parmesan cheese, for sprinkling
40g/1½oz herb and garlic soft cheese
150g/5oz firm goat's cheese, diced
6 egg whites, at room temperature
1.5ml/¼ tsp cream of tartar
salt and freshly ground black pepper

Serves 4–6

1 Melt the butter in a heavy saucepan. Add the flour and cook until golden, stirring continuously. Pour in half the milk, stirring vigorously until smooth to remove any lumps, then stir in the remaining milk and add the bay leaf. Season with a pinch of salt and plenty of pepper and nutmeg. Reduce the heat, cover and gently simmer the sauce for about 5 minutes, stirring occasionally.

2 Preheat the oven to 190°C/375°F/ Gas 5. Generously butter a 1.5 litre/ 2½ pint/6¼ cups soufflé dish and sprinkle the base and sides with Parmesan cheese.

3 Remove the sauce from the heat and discard the bay leaf. Stir in both cheeses until melted.

4 In a clean, grease-free bowl, using an electric mixer or balloon whisk, beat the egg whites slowly until they become frothy. Add the cream of tartar, increase the speed and continue beating until soft peaks form, then stiffer peaks.

5 Stir a spoonful of beaten egg white into the cheese sauce to lighten it, then pour the cheese sauce over the remaining whites. Using a metal spoon, gently fold the sauce into the whites until the mixtures are just combined, cutting down to the bottom, then along the side of the bowl and up to the top.

6 Gently pour the soufflé mixture into the prepared dish and bake for 25–30 minutes until puffed and golden brown. Serve at once.

GRILLED BRIE AND WALNUTS

This unusual cheese recipe will impress your guests with its sophisticated simplicity. You'll be pleased

to know that it requires almost no preparation.

INGREDIENTS

15g/½oz/1 tbsp butter, at room temperature
5ml/1 tsp Dijon mustard
675g/1½lb wheel of Brie or Camembert cheese
25g/1oz/¼ cup chopped walnuts
French stick, sliced and toasted to serve

Serves about 16–20

2 Sprinkle the surface with the walnuts and grill for 2–3 minutes longer until the nuts are golden. Take care not to burn them. Serve immediately with the French bread toasts. Allow your guests to help themselves, because the whole grilled Brie makes an attractive centrepiece to a festive table.

COOK'S TIP

A sharp serving knife will be appreciated by your guests as the grilled cheese will be quite sticky to cut. Offer a variety of crackers, crispbreads and savoury biscuits to serve with the cheese as an alternative to toasted French bread.

1 Preheat the grill. In a small bowl, cream together the butter and Dijon mustard, and spread evenly over the surface of the cheese. Transfer the cheese to a flameproof serving plate, and grill 12–15cm/4–6in from the heat for 3–4 minutes until the top just begins to bubble.

VARIATION

As an alternative to Brie or Camembert, try goat's cheese. For a change from walnuts, pine nuts could be used.

CHICKEN LIVER MOUSSE

This mousse makes an elegant yet easy first course. The onion marmalade make a delicious

accompaniment, along with a salad of chicory or other bitter leaves.

INGREDIENTS

175g/6oz/¾ cup butter, diced
1 small onion, finely chopped
1 garlic clove, finely chopped
450g/1lb chicken livers, trimmed
2.5ml/½ tsp dried thyme
30–45ml/2–3 tbsp brandy
salt and freshly ground black pepper
green salad, to serve

For the Onion Marmalade
25g/1oz/2 tbsp butter
450g/1lb red onions, thinly sliced
1 garlic clove, finely chopped
2.5ml/½ tsp dried thyme
30–45ml/2–3 tbsp red wine vinegar
15–30ml/1–2 tbsp clear honey
40g/1½oz/¼ cup sultanas (golden raisins)

Serves 6–8

1 In a heavy-based frying pan, melt 25g/1oz/2 tbsp of the butter. Add the onion and cook for 5–7 minutes until soft and golden, then add the garlic and cook for 1 minute more. Increase the heat and add the chicken livers, thyme, salt and black pepper. Cook for 3–5 minutes until the livers are coloured, stirring frequently; the livers should remain pink inside, but not raw. Add the brandy, stirring, and cook for a further minute.

2 Using a slotted spoon, transfer the livers to a food processor fitted with a metal blade. Pour in the cooking juices and process for 1 minute, or until smooth. With the machine running, add the remaining butter, a few pieces at a time, until it is incorporated.

3 Press the mousse mixture through a fine sieve (strainer) with a rubber spatula until it is smooth and creamy.

4 Line a 475ml/16fl oz/2 cup loaf tin with clear film, smoothing out wrinkles. Pour the mousse mixture into the lined tin. Cool, then cover and chill overnight, until firm.

5 To make the onion marmalade, fry the onions in the butter for 20 minutes until just coloured. Stir in the chopped garlic, thyme, vinegar, honey and sultanas and cook, covered, for 10–15 minutes, stirring occasionally, until the onions are completely soft and jam-like. Spoon into a serving bowl and allow to cool to room temperature.

6 To serve, dip the loaf tin into hot water for 5 seconds, wipe dry and invert. Lift off the tin, peel off the clear film and smooth the surface with a palette knife. Serve sliced, with the onion marmalade and a green salad.

FARMHOUSE PÂTÉ

This pâté is full of flavour and can be cut into slices for easy serving. You can make the pâté in individual dishes, or in a larger container if you are expecting an unspecified number of guests.

INGREDIENTS

8 slices rindless streaky (fatty) bacon
2 x 175g/6oz chicken breasts
225g/8oz chicken livers
1 onion, chopped
1 garlic clove, crushed
2.5ml/½ tsp salt
2.5ml/½ tsp freshly ground black pepper
5ml/1 tsp anchovy essence (paste)
5ml/1 tsp ground mace
15g/1 tbsp chopped fresh oregano
75g/3oz/1 cup fresh white breadcrumbs
1 egg
30ml/2 tbsp brandy
150ml/¼ pt/⅔ cup chicken stock
10ml/2 tsp gelatine

To Garnish
strips of pimento and black olives

Makes 450g/1lb

1 Preheat the oven to 160°C/325°F/ Gas 3. Press the bacon slices flat with a knife to stretch them slightly. Line the base and sides of each dish with bacon and neatly trim any excess off the edges.

2 Place the chicken breasts and livers, onion and garlic into a food processor. Process until smooth. Add the salt, pepper, anchovy essence, mace, oregano, breadcrumbs, egg and brandy. Process until the mixture is smooth.

3 Divide the mixture between the dishes. Cover the dishes with a double thickness of foil and stand them in a roasting tin. Add enough hot water to come halfway up the sides of the tin.

4 Bake in the centre of the oven for 1 hour or until firm. Remove the foil to release the steam. Place a weight on top of each dish to flatten until cool.

5 Pour the juices from each dish into a measuring jug and make up to 150ml/ ¼ pint/⅔ cup with chicken stock. Heat in a pan until boiling. Blend the gelatine with 30ml/2 tbsp water and pour into the stock, stirring. Allow to cool.

6 Garnish the pâté when cold, then spoon the gelatine mixture over the top. Chill until set. Cover with clear film.

Roquefort Tartlets

These can be made in shallow tartlet tins to serve hot as a first course. You could also make them

in tiny cocktail tins, to serve warm as bitesize snacks with a drink before a meal.

INGREDIENTS

175g/6oz/1½ cups plain
(all-purpose) flour
large pinch of salt
115g/4oz/½ cup butter
1 egg yolk
30ml/2 tbsp cold water

For the Filling
15g/½oz/1 tbsp butter
15g/1½oz/1 tbsp (all-purpose) flour
150ml/¼ pint/⅔ cup milk
115g/4oz Roquefort cheese, crumbled
150ml/¼ pint/⅔ cup double (heavy) cream
2.5ml/½ tsp dried mixed herbs
3 egg yolks
salt and freshly ground black pepper

1 To make the pastry, sift the flour and salt into a large mixing bowl and rub the butter in until it resembles breadcrumbs. Mix the egg with the water and stir into the flour to make a soft dough. Knead until smooth, wrap in clear film and chill for 30 minutes.

2 For the filling, melt the butter, stir in the flour and then the milk. Boil to thicken, stirring continuously. Off the heat, beat in the cheese and season. Allow to cool. Bring the cream and herbs to the boil. Reduce the mixture to 30ml/2 tbsp. Beat into the sauce with the egg yolks.

3 Preheat the oven to 190°C/375°F/ Gas 5. On a lightly floured work surface, roll out the pastry to a thickness of 3mm/⅛in. Stamp out rounds with a fluted or plain cutter and use to line the tartlet tins.

4 Divide the filling between the tartlets so they are two-thirds full. Stamp out smaller fluted rounds or star shapes and place one on top of each tartlet. Bake the tartlets for 20–25 minutes, or until they are golden brown.

Main Courses

For some, there can be no other main course than
turkey on Christmas Day, but an equally festive
main dish of pheasant, goose or duck will provide such
an attractive centrepiece that no one could object. To go even
further, who's to say that the seasonal celebration can't
be marked with a seafood alternative such as Sole with Prawns
and Mussels? Of course, venison, gammon or pork tenderloin
all have their appeal too, so the choice may be a difficult one.
If you're having a big crowd for dinner, you could give
your guests a choice and serve two main dishes such as
Roast Beef with Roasted Sweet Peppers and
Roast Pheasant with Port.

Roast Goose with Caramelized Apples

Choose a young goose with a pliable breast bone for the best possible flavour. This is a delicious meat when

enhanced by caramelized glazed apples and a citrus gravy.

INGREDIENTS

4.5–5.5kg/10–12lb goose, with giblets
(thawed overnight, if frozen)
salt and freshly ground black pepper

For the Apple and Nut Stuffing
225g/8oz/2 cups prunes
150ml/1¼ pint/⅔ cup port or red wine
675g/1½lb cooking apples, peeled, cored
and cubed
1 large onion, chopped
4 celery sticks, sliced
15ml/1 tbsp mixed dried herbs
finely grated rind of 1 orange
goose liver, chopped
450g/1lb pork sausage meat
(bulk sausage)
115g/4oz/1 cup chopped pecans
2 eggs

For the Caramelized Apples
50g/2oz/4 tbsp butter
60ml/4 tbsp redcurrant jelly
30ml/2 tbsp red wine vinegar
8 small dessert apples, peeled and cored

For the Gravy
30ml/2 tbsp plain (all-purpose) flour
600ml/1 pint/2½ cups giblet stock
juice of 1 orange

Serves 8

1 The day before they are needed, soak the prunes in the port or the red wine, pit them and cut each into four pieces. Reserve the port or red wine.

2 The next day, mix the prunes with all the remaining stuffing ingredients and season well. Moisten with half the reserved port.

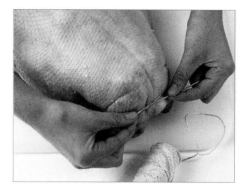

3 Preheat the oven to 200°C/400°F/ Gas 6. Stuff the neck-end of the goose, tuck the flap of skin under and secure it with a small skewer. Remove the excess fat from the cavity and add the stuffing. Do not pack too tightly or the skin may burst. Tie the legs together.

4 To cook, allow 15 minutes for each 450g/1lb. Put the bird on a rack in a roasting tin and rub the tin with salt. Prick the skin and roast for 30 minutes, then reduce the heat to 180°C/350°F/ Gas 4 and roast for the remaining cooking time. Pour off any fat produced during cooking into a bowl. The goose is cooked if the juices run clear when the thickest part of the thigh is pierced with a skewer. Pour cold water over the breast to crisp the skin.

5 Meanwhile, prepare the apples. Melt the butter, redcurrant jelly and vinegar in a small roasting tin or a shallow ovenproof dish. Put in the apples, baste them well and cook in the oven for 15–20 minutes. Baste the apples halfway through the cooking time. Do not cover them or they will collapse. Reserve the juices for a redcurrant glaze.

6 Lift the goose on to the serving dish and let it stand for 15 minutes before carving. Pour off the excess fat from the roasting tin, leaving any sediment behind in the bottom. Stir in the flour, cook gently until brown, and then blend in the stock. Bring to the boil, add the remaining reserved port, orange juice and seasoning. Simmer the gravy for 2–3 minutes. Strain into a gravy boat. Surround the goose with the caramelized apples and spoon over the redcurrant glaze.

ROAST TURKEY

Serve this classic Christmas roast turkey with all the traditional trimmings: stuffing balls,

bacon rolls, roast potatoes, Brussels sprouts and gravy.

INGREDIENTS

*4.5kg/10lb oven-ready turkey, with giblets
(thawed, if frozen)
1 large onion, peeled and studded with
6 whole cloves
50g/2oz/4 tbsp butter, softened
10 chipolata sausages
salt and freshly ground black pepper*

For the Stuffing
*225g/8oz rindless streaky (fatty)
bacon, chopped
1 large onion, finely chopped
450g/1lb pork sausage meat
25g/1oz/⅓ cup rolled oats
30ml/2 tbsp chopped fresh parsley
10ml/2 tsp dried mixed herbs
1 large egg, beaten
115g/4oz dried apricots, finely chopped*

For the Gravy
*25g/1oz/2 tbsp plain (all-purpose) flour
450ml/¾ pint/1⅞ cups giblet stock*

Serves 8

1 Preheat the oven to 200°C/400°F/ Gas 6. Adjust the spacing of the shelves if necessary. To make the stuffing, cook the bacon and the onion together over a gentle heat in a heavy-based frying pan until the bacon is crisp and the onion is tender but not browned. Transfer the cooked bacon and onion to a large mixing bowl and add in all the remaining stuffing ingredients. Season with salt and freshly ground black pepper and mix well to blend.

2 Stuff the neck-end of the turkey only, tucking the flap of skin under and securing it with a small skewer or stitching it in place with a large needle and thread. Do not overstuff the turkey or the skin will burst during cooking. Reserve any remaining stuffing and set aside.

3 Put the onion studded with cloves in the body cavity of the turkey and tie the legs together with string to hold them in place. Weigh the stuffed bird and calculate the cooking time: allow 15 minutes per 450g/1lb plus 15 minutes extra. Place the turkey in a large roasting tin.

4 Brush the turkey all over with the butter and season well with salt and pepper. Cover it loosely with foil and cook it for 30 minutes. Baste the turkey with the pan juices. Then lower the oven temperature to 180°C/350°F/ Gas 4 and continue to cook for the remainder of the calculated time. Baste the turkey every 30 minutes or so.

5 With wet hands, shape the remaining stuffing into small balls or pack it into a greased ovenproof dish. Cook in the oven for 20 minutes, or until golden brown or crisp. About 20 minutes before the end of cooking, put the chipolata sausages into an ovenproof dish and put them in the oven. Remove the foil from the turkey for the last hour of cooking and baste. The turkey is cooked if the juices run clear when the thickest part of the thigh is pierced with a skewer.

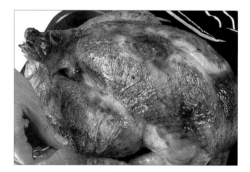

6 Transfer the turkey to a serving plate, cover it with foil and let it stand for 15 minutes before carving. To make the gravy, spoon off the fat from the roasting pan, leaving the meat juices. Blend in the flour and cook for 2 minutes. Gradually stir in the stock and bring to the boil. Check the seasoning and pour into a sauce boat. Remove the skewer and pour any juices into the gravy. To serve, surround the turkey with chipolata sausages, bacon rolls and stuffing.

ROAST PHEASANT WITH PORT

Roasting the pheasant in foil helps to keep the flesh particularly moist and succulent.

This recipe is best for very young birds, and if you have a choice and an obliging butcher you

should request the more tender female birds.

INGREDIENTS

vegetable oil
2 oven-ready hen pheasants
(about 675g/1½lb each)
50g/2oz/4 tbsp unsalted butter, softened
8 fresh thyme sprigs
2 bay leaves
6 streaky bacon (fatty) rashers
15 ml/1 tbsp plain (all-purpose) flour
175ml/6fl oz/¾ cup game or chicken stock
15ml/1 tbsp redcurrant jelly
45–60ml/ 3–4 tbsp port
freshly ground black pepper

Serves 4

1 Preheat the oven to 230°C/450°F/ Gas 8. Line a large roasting tin with a sheet of strong foil that is large enough to wrap around and securely enclose both of the pheasants. Lightly brush the foil all over with a little vegetable oil.

2 Wipe the pheasants with damp kitchen paper and remove any skin or fat. With your fingertips, loosen the skin of the breasts. With a small palette knife, spread the butter between the skin and the breast meat of each bird. Tie the legs securely with string then lay the thyme sprigs and a bay leaf over the breast of each bird.

3 Arrange the bacon rashers over the pheasant breasts so that they are almost completely covered, place the birds in the foil-lined tin and season with plenty of ground black pepper. Bring together the long ends of the foil, fold over securely to enclose so that all the juices are retained in the foil package, then twist firmly together to seal.

4 Roast the birds for 20 minutes then reduce the oven temperature to 190°C/375°F/Gas 5 and cook for a further 40 minutes. Uncover the birds and roast 10–15 minutes more or until they are browned and the juices run clear when the thigh of each of the birds is pierced with a skewer. Transfer the birds to a board and leave to stand, covered with clean foil, for 10 minutes before carving.

5 Pour the juices from the foil into the roasting tin and skim off any fat. Sprinkle the flour into the juices and cook over a medium heat, stirring continuously until the mixture is smooth. Whisk in the stock and the redcurrant jelly and bring to the boil. Simmer until the sauce thickens slightly, adding more stock if needed, then stir in the port and adjust the seasoning to taste. Strain the sauce and serve at once, with the pheasants.

VARIATION

Other game birds that would be suitable for this type of cooking include guinea fowl and partridge, but try to get tender young birds.

DUCK WITH ORANGE SAUCE

Commercially raised ducks tend to have more fat than wild ducks. In this recipe, the initial slow cooking

and pricking the skin of the duck help to draw out the excess fat.

INGREDIENTS

2kg/4½lb duck
2 oranges
100g/3½oz/½ cup caster (superfine) sugar
90ml/6 tbsp white wine vinegar or
cider vinegar
120ml/4fl oz/½ cup Grand Marnier or
orange liqueur
salt and freshly ground black pepper
watercress and orange slices, to garnish

Serves 2–3

1 Preheat the oven to 150ºC/300ºF/ Gas 2. Trim off all the excess over-hanging fat and skin from the duck and prick the skin all over with a fork or skewer. Generously season the duck inside and out with salt and freshly ground black pepper, and tie the legs together with string to hold them in place.

2 Place the duck on a rack in a large roasting tin. Cover tightly with foil and cook in the preheated oven for 1½ hours. Using a vegetable peeler, remove the rind in wide strips from the oranges, then stack up two or three strips at a time and slice into very thin julienne strips. Squeeze the juice from the oranges and set it aside.

3 Place the caster sugar and vinegar in a small heavy-based saucepan and stir to dissolve the sugar. Boil over a high heat, without stirring, until the mixture is a rich caramel colour. Remove the pan from the heat and, standing well back, carefully add the freshly squeezed orange juice, pouring it down the side of the pan. Swirl the pan to blend, then bring back to the boil and add the orange rind and liqueur. Simmer for 2–3 minutes.

4 Remove the duck from the oven and pour off all the fat from the roasting tin. Raise the oven temperature to 200ºC/ 400ºF/Gas 6.

5 Roast the duck, uncovered, for 25–30 minutes, basting three or four times with the caramel mixture, until the duck is golden brown and the juices run clear when the thigh is pierced with a skewer.

6 Pour the juices from the cavity into the casserole and transfer the duck to a carving board. Cover loosely with foil and leave to stand for 10–15 minutes. Pour the roasting juices into the pan with the rest of the caramel mixture, skim off the fat and simmer gently. Serve the duck with the orange sauce, garnished with sprigs of watercress and orange slices.

VARIATION

Traditionally, roasted duck is served with a fruity sauce to offset the richness, as in this recipe. A cherry sauce is a good alternative to an orange sauce and can be made using either frozen or canned cherries.

ROAST LEG OF VENISON

The marinade for this recipe forms the base for a deliciously tangy, slightly sweet sauce that

complements the richness of roasted venison perfectly.

INGREDIENTS

1 onion, chopped
1 carrot, chopped
1 celery stick, chopped
3 or 4 garlic cloves, crushed
4–6 fresh parsley sprigs
4–6 fresh thyme sprigs
2 bay leaves
15ml/1 tbsp peppercorns, lightly crushed
750ml/1¼ pints/3 cups red wine
60ml/4 tbsp vegetable oil, plus more
for brushing
1 young venison haunch, about 2.75kg/
6lb, trimmed
30ml/2 tbsp plain (all-purpose) flour
250ml/8fl oz/1 cup beef stock
1 unwaxed orange
1 unwaxed lemon
60ml/4 tbsp redcurrant or raspberry jelly
60ml/4 tbsp ruby port or Madeira
15ml/1 tbsp cornflour (cornstarch),
blended with 30ml/2 tbsp water
15ml/1 tbsp red wine vinegar
fresh herbs, to garnish

Serves 6–8

1 Place the onion, carrot, celery, garlic, parsley, thyme, bay leaves, peppercorns, wine and oil in a dish that is large enough to hold the venison, then add the venison and turn to coat. Cover the dish with clear film and leave to marinate in the refrigerator for 2–3 days, turning occasionally.

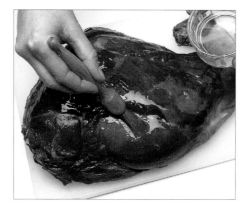

2 Preheat the oven to 180°C/350°F/ Gas 4. Remove the meat from its marinade and pour the marinade into a saucepan. Pat the meat dry, then brush with a little oil and wrap in foil.

3 Roast the venison for 15–20 minutes per 450g/1lb for rare to medium meat. About 25 minutes before the end of the cooking time, remove the foil, sprinkle the venison with the flour and baste.

4 Add the stock to the marinade and boil until reduced by half, then strain and set aside.

5 Using a vegetable peeler, remove the rind from the orange and half the lemon. Cut the pieces into thin julienne strips. Bring a saucepan of water to the boil and add the orange and lemon strips. Simmer them for 5 minutes, then drain and rinse under cold water.

6 Squeeze the juice of the orange into a medium saucepan. Add the redcurrant or raspberry jelly and cook over a low heat until melted, then stir in the port or Madeira and the reduced marinade and simmer gently for 10 minutes, stirring.

7 Stir the blended cornflour mixture into the marinade and cook, stirring frequently with a whisk, until the sauce is slightly thickened. Add the vinegar and the orange and lemon strips and simmer for a further 2–3 minutes. Keep the sauce warm, stirring occasionally, to keep the fruit strips separated.

8 Transfer the venison to a board and allow to stand, loosely covered with foil, for 10 minutes before carving. Garnish with your chosen fresh herbs and serve with the sauce.

FILET MIGNON WITH MUSHROOMS

This haute cuisine French dish was originally made with truffle slices, but large mushroom caps

are less expensive and look just as attractive, especially when they are fluted.

INGREDIENTS

4 thin slices white bread
120g/4oz pâté de foie gras or mousse de
foie gras
4 large white (button) mushroom caps
70g/2½oz/5 tbsp butter
10ml/2 tsp vegetable oil
4 fillet steaks, about 2.5cm/1in thick
45–60ml/3–4 tbsp Madeira or port
125ml/4fl oz/½ cup beef stock
watercress sprigs, to garnish

Serves 4

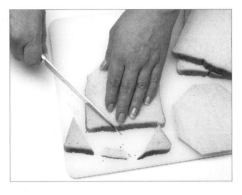

1 Cut the bread into rounds about the same diameter as the steaks, using a large round cutter or by cutting into squares, then cutting off the corners. Toast the bread and spread with the foie gras, dividing it evenly. Place the bread on warmed plates.

2 Flute the mushroom caps using the edge of a knife blade. Melt about 25g/1oz/1 tbsp of the butter and sauté them until golden. Transfer the mushrooms to a plate and keep warm.

3 In the same pan, melt another 25g/1oz/1 tbsp of the butter with the oil, swirling to combine. When the butter just begins to brown, add the steaks and cook for 6–8 minutes, turning once, until cooked as preferred (medium-rare meat will still be slightly soft when pressed, medium will be springy and well-done firm). Place the steaks on the bread and top with the cooked mushroom caps.

4 Add the Madeira or port to the pan and boil for 20–30 seconds. Add the stock and boil until the liquid is reduced by three-quarters. Swirl in the remaining butter. Pour a little sauce over each steak, then garnish with sprigs of watercress.

CHATEAUBRIAND WITH BÉARNAISE SAUCE

Chateaubriand is a lean and tender cut of beef from the thick centre of the fillet that is pounded to give it its characteristic shape. This portion is usually served for two people.

INGREDIENTS

150g/5oz/⅔ cup butter, cut into pieces
25ml/1½ tbsp tarragon vinegar
25ml/1½ tbsp dry white wine
1 shallot, finely chopped
2 egg yolks
450g/1lb beef fillet, about 12.5–15cm/
5–6in long, cut from the thickest part of
the fillet
15ml/1 tbsp vegetable oil
salt and freshly ground black pepper
Sautéed Potatoes, to serve

Serves 2

1 To make the sauce, clarify the butter by melting it in a saucepan over a low heat; do not boil. Skim off any foam and set aside.

2 Put the vinegar, wine and shallot in a small heavy saucepan over a high heat and boil to reduce until almost evaporated. Remove from the heat and cool slightly. Add the egg and whisk for 1 minute. Place the saucepan over a very low heat and whisk until the yolk mixture begins to thicken and the whisk begins to leave tracks, then remove the pan from the heat.

3 Whisk in the butter, slowly at first, then more quickly, until the sauce thickens. Season and keep warm.

4 Place the meat between two sheets of greaseproof paper or clear film and pound with the flat side of a meat pounder or roll with a rolling pin to flatten until the meat is about 4cm/1½in thick. Season with plenty of salt and pepper.

5 Heat the vegetable oil in a heavy-based frying pan over a medium-high heat. Add the meat and cook for about 10–12 minutes, turning once, until cooked as preferred (medium-rare meat will be slightly soft when pressed, medium will be springy and well-done will be firm).

6 Transfer the steak to a wooden board and, using a very sharp kitchen knife, carve the meat in thin, diagonal slices. If you prefer a smooth sauce, strain off the shallots through a fine sieve (strainer) then serve the Béarnaise sauce with the steak, accompanied by sautéed potatoes and extra sauce on the side.

ROAST BEEF WITH ROASTED SWEET PEPPERS

This substantial and warming dish makes an ideal dinner for cold winter nights.

INGREDIENTS

1.5kg/3–3½lb piece of sirloin
15ml/1 tbsp olive oil
450g/1lb small red (bell) peppers
115g/4oz/¾ cup mushrooms
175g/6oz thick-sliced pancetta, cubed
50g/2oz/2 tbsp plain (all-purpose) flour
150ml/¼ pint/⅔ cup full-bodied red wine
300ml/½ pint/1¼ cups beef stock
30ml/2 tbsp Marsala
10ml/2 tsp mixed dried herbs
salt and freshly ground black pepper

Serves 8

1 Preheat the oven to 190°C/375°F/ Gas 5. Season the meat. Heat the oil in a pan, then brown the meat. Place in a roasting tin and cook for 1¼ hours.

2 Put the red peppers in the oven to roast for 20 minutes (or roast for 45 minutes if using larger peppers).

3 Near the end of the meat's cooking time, prepare the gravy. Roughly chop the mushroom caps and stems.

4 Heat the pan again and add the pancetta. Cook until the fat runs from the meat. Add the flour to the pan and cook for a few minutes until browned.

5 Stir in the red wine and stock and bring to the boil. Lower the heat then add the Marsala, herbs and seasoning.

6 Add the mushrooms and heat through. Remove the sirloin from the oven and leave to stand for 10 minutes. Serve with the peppers and hot gravy.

ROAST STUFFED LAMB

This lamb is stuffed with a tempting blend of kidneys, spinach and rice.

INGREDIENTS

1.8–2kg/4–4½ lb boneless leg or shoulder of lamb (not tied)
25g/1oz/2 tbsp butter, softened
15–30ml/1–2tbsp plain (all-purpose) flour
120ml/4fl oz/½ cup white wine
250ml/8fl oz/1 cup chicken or beef stock
salt and freshly ground black pepper
watercress, to garnish

For the Stuffing
65g/2½oz/5 tbsp butter
1 small onion, finely chopped
1 garlic clove, finely chopped
50g/2oz/⅓ cup long grain rice
150ml/¼ pint/⅔ cup chicken stock
2.5ml/½ tsp dried thyme
4 lamb's kidneys, halved and cored
275g/10oz young spinach leaves
salt and freshly ground black pepper

Serves 6–8

1 To make the stuffing, melt 25g/1oz/ 2 tbsp of the butter in a saucepan over a medium heat. Add the onion and cook for 2–3 minutes, then add the garlic and rice and cook for 1–2 minutes, stirring constantly. Add the stock, salt and pepper and thyme and bring to the boil, stirring occasionally, then reduce the heat and cook for 18 minutes, covered, until tender and the liquid is absorbed. Transfer to a bowl and fluff with a fork.

2 Melt 25g/1oz/2 tbsp of the remaining butter. Add the kidneys and cook for 2–3 minutes, turning once, until lightly browned but still pink inside. Cool. Cut the kidneys into pieces and add to the rice, season with salt and pepper and toss to combine.

3 Heat the remaining butter over a medium heat until foaming. Add the spinach leaves and cook for 1–2 minutes until wilted, drain off excess liquid, then transfer the leaves to a plate and leave to cool.

4 Preheat the oven to 190°C/375°F/ Gas 5. Lay the meat skin-side down on a work surface and season. Spread the spinach leaves over the surface, then spread the stuffing over the spinach. Roll up the meat and use a skewer to close the seam. Tie the meat at intervals, then place in a roasting tin, spread with the butter and season.

5 Roast for 1½–2 hours until the juices run slightly pink when pierced with a skewer, or until a meat thermometer inserted into the thickest part of the meat registers 57–60°C/135–140°F (for medium-rare to medium). Transfer the meat to a carving board, cover with foil and leave for about 20 minutes.

6 Skim off the fat from the roasting tin. Place the tin over a medium heat and bring to the boil. Sprinkle over the flour and cook for 3 minutes until browned, stirring and scraping the base of the tin. Whisk in the wine and stock and bring to the boil. Cook for 5 minutes until the sauce thickens. Season and strain. Garnish the meat with watercress and serve with the gravy and potatoes.

BAKED GAMMON WITH CUMBERLAND SAUCE

Serve this delicious cooked meat and sauce either hot or cold. The tangy orange sauce

offsets the sweetness of the gammon perfectly.

INGREDIENTS

*2.25kg/5lb smoked or unsmoked
gammon joint
1 onion
1 carrot
1 celery stick
bouquet garni sachet
6 peppercorns*

For the Glaze
*whole cloves
50g/2oz/4 tbsp soft light brown or
demerara sugar
30ml/2 tbsp golden syrup
5ml/1 tsp English mustard powder*

For the Cumberland Sauce
*juice and shredded rind of 1 orange
30ml/2 tbsp lemon juice
120ml/4fl oz/½ cup port or red wine
60ml/4 tbsp redcurrant jelly*

Serves 8–10

1 Soak the gammon overnight in a cool place in enough cold water to cover. Discard this water. Put the joint into a large pan and cover it with more cold water. Bring the water to the boil slowly and skim off any scum that rises to the surface.

2 Add the vegetables and seasonings, cover the pan and simmer over a gentle heat for 2 hours.

3 Leave the meat to cool in the liquid for 30 minutes. Remove it and strip off the skin with the help of a knife (use rubber gloves if the gammon is hot).

4 Score the fat in diamonds with a sharp knife and stick a clove in the centre of each diamond.

5 Preheat the oven to 180°C/350°F/ Gas 4. Heat the sugar, golden syrup and mustard powder in a small pan to melt them. Place the gammon in a roasting tin and spoon over the glaze. Bake it until golden, about 20 minutes. Put it under a hot grill, if needed, to get a good colour. Stand in a warm place for 15 minutes before carving.

6 For the sauce, put the orange and lemon juice into a pan with the port or red wine and jelly, and heat to melt the jelly. Pour boiling water on to the orange rind, drain, and add to the sauce. Cook for 2 minutes. Serve in a jug.

Tenderloin of Pork Wrapped in Bacon

This easy-to-carve "joint" is served with a tasty onion and prune gravy. The pickling onions

add an interesting piquancy to the sauce.

INGREDIENTS

1.2kg/2½lb pork fillet
225g/8oz rindless streaky (fatty) bacon
25g/1oz/2 tbsp butter
150ml/¼ pint/⅔ cup red wine

For the Prune Stuffing
25g/1oz/2 tbsp butter
1 onion, very finely chopped
115g/4oz mushrooms, finely chopped
*4 ready-to-eat prunes, stoned (pitted)
and chopped*
10ml/2 tsp mixed dried herbs
115g/4oz/2 cups fresh white breadcrumbs
1 egg
salt and freshly ground black pepper

To Finish
16 ready-to-eat prunes
150ml/¼ pint/⅔ cup red wine
16 pickling (pearl) onions
30ml/2 tbsp plain (all-purpose) flour
300ml/½ pint/1¼ cups chicken stock

Serves 8

1 Preheat the oven to 180°C/350°F/ Gas 4. Trim the fillets and cut each lengthways, three-quarters of the way through, open them out and flatten.

2 For the stuffing, melt the butter and cook the onion, add the mushrooms and cook for 5 minutes. Transfer to a bowl. Add the remaining stuffing ingredients. Spread over two of the fillets and sandwich together with the third fillet.

3 Stretch each rasher of bacon with the back of a large knife.

4 Overlap the rashers across the meat. Cut lengths of string and lay them at 2cm/¾in intervals over the bacon. Cover with foil and hold in place. Roll the "joint" over. Fold the bacon over the meat and tie the string to secure them in place. Roll the "joint" back on to the bacon joins and remove the foil.

5 Place in a roasting tin and spread the butter over the joint. Pour the wine around the meat and cook for 1¼ hours, basting occasionally with the liquid in the roasting tin, until browned. Simmer the remaining prunes in the red wine until tender. Boil the onions in salted water for 10 minutes, or until just tender. Drain and add to the prunes.

6 Transfer the pork to a serving plate, remove the string, cover loosely with foil and leave to stand for 10–15 minutes, before carving into slices. Remove any fat from the roasting tin, add the flour to the sediment and juices and cook gently for 2–3 minutes. Then blend in the stock, bring to the boil and simmer for 5 minutes. Adjust the seasoning to taste. Strain the gravy on to the prunes and onions, reheat and serve in a sauce boat with a ladle.

SOLE WITH PRAWNS AND MUSSELS

This luxurious dish is a classic seafood recipe. It is a true feast for fish lovers at any time

of the year and would make a welcome change at Christmas.

INGREDIENTS

75g/3oz/6 tbsp butter
8 shallots, finely chopped
300ml/½ pint/1¼ cups dry white wine
1kg/2¼lb mussels, scrubbed
and debearded
225g/8oz button (white)
mushrooms, quartered
250ml/8fl oz/1 cup fish stock
12 skinless lemon or Dover sole fillets,
about 75–150g/3–5oz each
30ml/2 tbsp plain (all-purpose) flour
60ml/4 tbsp double (heavy) cream
225g/8oz/2 cups cooked, peeled
prawns (shrimp)
salt and white pepper
fresh parsley sprigs, to garnish

Serves 6

3 Transfer the mussels to a large bowl. Strain the cooking liquid through a muslin-lined sieve (strainer) and reserve. When they are cool enough to handle, remove the mussels from their shells, reserving a few for the garnish. Set aside.

6 Melt the remaining butter in a small saucepan over a medium heat. Add the flour and cook for 1–2 minutes, stirring constantly; do not allow the mixture to brown. Whisk in the reduced fish cooking liquid, the reserved mussel liquid and any liquid from the fish, then bring to the boil, stirring constantly.

1 Tap each mussel sharply and discard any that do not close. In a large heavy flameproof casserole, melt 15g/½oz/1 tbsp of the butter over a medium-high heat. Add half the shallots and cook or 2 minutes until softened, but not browned. Stir the shallots frequently. Add the white wine and bring quickly to the boil, then add the mussels and cover the pan tightly.

2 Cook the mussels over a high heat. shaking the pan now and then, for 4–5 minutes until the shells open. Discard any mussels that do not open.

4 Melt half the remaining butter in a frying pan. Add the remaining shallots and cook for 2 minutes until just softened, stirring frequently. Add the mushrooms and fish stock and bring just to simmering point. Season the fish fillets with salt and pepper.

5 Fold or roll them and slide gently into the stock. Cover and poach for 5–7 minutes until the flesh is opaque. Transfer the fillets to a warmed serving dish and cover tightly to keep warm. Increase the heat and boil the liquid until it has reduced by one-third.

7 Reduce the heat to medium-low and cook the sauce for 5–7 minutes, stirring frequently. Whisk in the crème fraîche or double cream and keep stirring over a low heat until the sauce is well blended. Adjust the seasoning to taste, then add the reserved mussels and the cooked prawns to the sauce.

8 Cook gently for 2–3 minutes to heat through, then spoon the sauce over the fish and serve garnished with fresh parsley sprigs and the mussels in their shells.

LOBSTER THERMIDOR

Lobster Thermidor is a rich and delicious dish that is luxurious enough

to serve at Christmas-time. Serve one lobster per person as a main course or

one filled shell each for a starter.

INGREDIENTS

2 live lobsters, about 675g/1½lb each
20g/¾oz/1½ tbsp butter
30ml/2 tbsp plain (all-purpose) flour
30ml/2 tbsp brandy
120ml/4fl oz/½ cup milk
90ml/6 tbsp whipping cream
15ml/1 tbsp Dijon mustard
lemon juice, salt and white pepper
grated Parmesan cheese, for sprinkling
fresh parsley and dill, to garnish

Serves 2–4

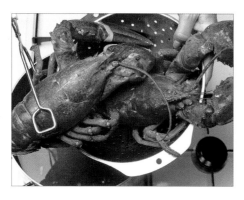

1 Boil the lobsters in a large saucepan of salted water for 8–10 minutes.

2 Cut the lobsters in half lengthways and discard the dark sac behind the eyes, then pull out the string-like intestine from the tail. Remove the meat from the shells, reserving the coral and liver, then rinse the shells thoroughly under running water and wipe dry. Cut the meat into bitesize pieces.

3 Melt the butter in a heavy saucepan over a medium-high heat. Stir in the flour and cook, stirring, until slightly golden. Pour in the brandy and milk, whisking vigorously until smooth, then whisk in the cream and mustard.

4 Push the lobster coral and liver through a sieve into the sauce and whisk briskly to blend. Reduce the heat to low and simmer gently for about 10 minutes, stirring frequently, until thickened. Season the sauce with salt, if needed, then add pepper and lemon juice.

5 Preheat the grill. Arrange the lobster shells in a gratin dish or shallow flameproof baking dish.

6 Stir the lobster meat into the sauce and divide the mixture evenly among the shells. Sprinkle with Parmesan cheese and grill until golden. Serve piping hot, garnished with fresh herbs.

Salmon with Herb Butter

Here, salmon is simply roasted in foil with a delicious dill butter, which will impart a

wonderfully delicate flavour to the fish and offset the rich taste of the salmon. Serve simply

with new potatoes and a fresh green vegetable.

INGREDIENTS
*50g/2oz/1/4 cup butter, softened, plus
extra for greasing
finely grated rind of 1 lemon
15ml/1 tbsp lemon juice
15ml/1 tbsp chopped fresh dill
4 salmon steaks
2 lemon slices, halved
4 sprigs of fresh dill
salt and ground black pepper*

Serves 4

1 Place the butter, lemon rind, lemon juice and chopped fresh dill in a small bowl and mix together with a fork until blended. Season to taste with salt and ground black pepper.

2 Spoon the butter on to a small piece of baking parchment and roll up, smoothing with your hands into a sausage shape. Twist the ends tightly, wrap in clear film (plastic wrap) and put in the freezer for 20 minutes, until firm.

3 Meanwhile, preheat the oven to 190°C/375°F/Gas 5. Cut out four squares of foil to encase the salmon steaks and grease with butter. Place a salmon steak into the centre of each.

4 Remove the herb butter from the freezer and use a sharp knife to slice into eight rounds. Place two rounds on top of each salmon steak with a lemon slice in the centre and a sprig of dill on top. Lift up and crinkle the edges of the foil together until well sealed. Place the foil-wrapped salmon parcels on a baking tray.

5 Bake for 20 minutes then place the parcels on plates. Open the parcels and slide out the salmon with the juices.

Vegetarian Dishes and Vegetables

$\mathcal{I}$n any Christmas celebration today, it's likely that

you'll have some vegetarian guests, and they'll appreciate

more than just the leftover vegetables. Many recipes here, such

as Vegetarian Christmas Pie or Cheese, Rice and Vegetable

Strudel can stand alone as vegetarian main courses or can

make a wonderful accompaniment to the turkey in place of

traditional vegetables and potatoes. Many delicious vegetarian

recipes are found in other countries, and Spiced Vegetable

Couscous will bring an international element to the Christmas

table. And what would Christmas be without Brussels sprouts,

Hasselback Potatoes and Parsnip and Chestnut Croquettes?

All are extra-special dishes for the festive table.

VEGETARIAN CHRISTMAS PIE

A sophisticated mushroom flan with a cheese-soufflé topping. Serve hot with cranberry relish

and Festive Brussels Sprouts with chestnuts and carrots.

INGREDIENTS

225g/8oz/2 cups plain (all-purpose) flour
175g/6oz/¾ cup butter
10ml/2 tsp paprika
115g/4oz Parmesan cheese, grated
1 egg, beaten with 15ml/1 tbsp cold water
15ml/1 tbsp Dijon mustard

For the Filling
25g/1oz/2 tbsp butter
1 onion, finely chopped
1–2 garlic cloves, crushed
350g/12oz/5 cups mushrooms, chopped
10ml/2 tsp mixed dried herbs
15ml/1 tbsp chopped fresh parsley
50g/2oz/1 cup fresh white breadcrumbs
salt and freshly ground black pepper

For the Cheese Topping
25g/1oz/2 tbsp butter
25g/1oz/2 tbsp plain (all-purpose) flour
300ml/½pint/1¼ cups milk
25g/1oz Parmesan cheese, grated
75g/3oz Cheddar cheese, grated
1.5ml/¼ tsp English mustard powder
1 egg, separated

Serves 8

1 To make the pastry, sift the flour into a bowl and rub in the butter until the mixture resembles fine breadcrumbs. Stir in the paprika and the Parmesan cheese. Bind to a soft pliable dough with the egg and water. Knead until smooth, wrap in clear film and chill for 30 minutes.

2 For the filling, melt the butter and cook the onion until tender. Add the garlic and mushrooms and cook, uncovered, for 5 minutes, stirring occasionally. Increase the heat and drive off any liquid in the pan. Remove the pan from the heat and stir in the dried herbs, parsley, breadcrumbs and seasoning. Allow to cool.

3 Preheat the oven to 190°C/375°F/ Gas 5. Put a baking tray in the oven. On a lightly floured surface, roll out the pastry and use it to line a 23cm/ 9in loose-based flan tin, pressing the pastry well into the edges and making a narrow rim around the top edge. Chill for 20 minutes.

4 For the cheese topping, melt the butter in a pan, stir in the flour and cook for 2 minutes. Gradually blend in the milk. Bring to the boil to thicken and simmer for 2–3 minutes. Remove the pan from the heat and stir in the cheeses, mustard powder and egg yolk, and season well. Beat until smooth. Whisk the egg white until it holds soft peaks. Then, using a metal spoon, fold the egg white into the topping.

5 To assemble the pie, spread the Dijon mustard evenly over the base of the flan case with a palette knife. Spoon in the mushroom filling and level the surface by tapping the case firmly on the work surface.

6 Pour over the cheese topping and bake the pie on the hot baking tray for 35–45 minutes until the topping is set and golden. If you tap on the bottom of the flan case it should sound hollow. Serve at once or freeze until needed.

CHEESE, RICE AND VEGETABLE STRUDEL

Based on a traditional Russian recipe called "Koulibiac", this dish makes a perfect vegetarian

main course or, for meat-eaters, a welcome accompaniment to cold leftover turkey or sliced ham.

INGREDIENTS

175g/6oz/⅞ cup long grain rice
25g/1oz/2 tbsp butter
1–2 leeks, thinly sliced
350g/12oz/5 cups mushrooms, sliced
*225g/8oz Gruyère or Cheddar
cheese, grated*
225g/8oz feta cheese, cubed
30ml/2 tbsp currants
*50g/2oz/½ cup chopped almonds or
hazelnuts, toasted*
30ml/2 tbsp chopped fresh parsley
*275g/10oz packet frozen filo
pastry, thawed*
30ml/2 tbsp olive oil
salt and freshly ground black pepper

Serves 8

1 Cook the rice in boiling, salted water for 10–12 minutes, until tender but still with a little "bite". Drain, rinse under cold running water and set aside to drain again. Melt the butter and cook the leeks and mushrooms for 5 minutes more. Transfer to a large bowl and set aside until the vegetables have cooled.

2 Add the well-drained rice, the cheeses, currants, toasted almonds or hazelnuts, chopped fresh parsley and season to taste. (You may not need to add very much salt as the feta cheese is very salty.)

3 Preheat the oven to 190°C/375°F/ Gas 5. Cover the filo pastry with clear film and a clean damp cloth while you work, to stop it drying out.

4 Lay a sheet of filo pastry on a large piece of greaseproof paper and brush it with oil. Lay a second sheet on top, overlapping the first by 2.5cm/1in. Put another sheet with its long side running at right angles to the first two. Lay a fourth sheet in the same way, overlapping by 2.5cm/1in. Continue in this way, so that the join between the two sheets runs in the opposite direction for each layer.

5 Place the filling mixture along the centre of the pastry sheet and carefully shape it with your hands into a rectangle that measures approximately 10 x 30cm/4 x 12in.

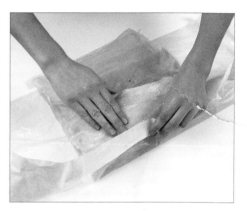

6 Fold the layers of filo pastry over the filling and carefully roll it over, with the help of the greaseproof paper, so that the join ends up being hidden on the underside of the strudel.

7 Lift the strudel on to a greased baking tray and gently tuck the edges under, so that the filling does not escape during cooking. Brush with oil and bake for 30–40 minutes, until golden-brown and crisp. Allow the strudel to stand for 5 minutes before cutting into thick slices. Serve at once or freeze until needed.

COOK'S TIP

The traditional Koulibiac dish has slices of hard-boiled egg as an ingredient in the filling – you could add it if you like.

CHEESE AND SPINACH FLAN

This flan freezes well and can be reheated. It makes an excellent addition to a festive buffet party

or a substantial main course for a vegetarian meal.

INGREDIENTS

115g/4oz/½ cup butter
225g/8oz/2 cups plain (all-purpose) flour
2.5ml/½ tsp English mustard powder
2.5ml/½ tsp paprika
large pinch of salt
115g/4oz/1 cup grated Cheddar cheese
45–60ml/3–4 tbsp cold water
1 egg, beaten, to glaze

For the Filling
450g/1lb frozen spinach
1 onion, chopped
pinch of grated nutmeg
225g/8oz/1 cup cottage cheese
2 large eggs
50g/2oz Parmesan cheese, grated
150ml/¼ pint/⅔ cup single (light) cream
salt and freshly ground black pepper

Serves 8

1 Using your fingertips, rub the butter into the flour until it resembles fine breadcrumbs. Rub in the next four ingredients. Alternatively, process in a food processor. Bind to a dough with the cold water. Knead until smooth and pliable, wrap in clear film and chill for about 30 minutes.

2 Put the spinach and onion in a pan, cover, and cook slowly. Increase the heat to drive off any water. Season with salt, pepper and nutmeg. Turn the spinach into a bowl, cool slightly. Add the remaining filling ingredients.

3 Preheat the oven to 200°C/400°F/ Gas 6. Put a baking tray in the oven to preheat. Cut one-third off the pastry for the lid. Roll out the remaining pastry and line a 23cm/9in loose-based flan tin. Press the pastry into the edges and make a lip around the top edge. Remove excess. Pour the filling into the case.

4 Roll out the remaining pastry and cut it with a lattice pastry cutter. Open the lattice, and, with a rolling pin, lay it over the flan. Brush the joins with egg. Press the edges together, trim off any excess. Brush with egg and bake for 40 minutes, until golden. Serve hot or cold.

CHESTNUT AND MUSHROOM LOAF

You can prepare this dish ahead, freezing it unbaked. Thaw at room temperature overnight

before baking. This dish would be ideal as a festive main course for vegetarians.

INGREDIENTS

*45ml/3 tbsp olive oil, plus extra
for brushing
2 medium onions, chopped
2 cloves garlic, chopped
75g/3oz/1¼ cups chopped button
(white) mushrooms
100ml/4fl oz/½ cup red wine
225g/8oz can unsweetened chestnut purée
50g/2oz/1 cup fresh
wholemeal breadcrumbs
salt and freshly ground black pepper
75g/3oz/¾ cup fresh cranberries, plus
extra to decorate
450g/1lb pastry
flour for dusting
1 small egg, beaten, to glaze*

Serves 8

1 Preheat the oven to 190°C/375°F/ Gas 5. Heat the oil in a pan and fry the onions over a medium heat until they are translucent. This will take about 7–8 minutes. Add the chopped garlic and mushrooms and fry for a further 3 minutes. Pour in the wine, stir well and simmer over a low heat until it has evaporated, stirring occasionally. Remove from the heat, stir in the chestnut purée and the breadcrumbs and season to taste with salt and pepper. Set aside.

2 Simmer the cranberries in a little water for 5 minutes until they start to pop then drain and leave to cool.

3 Lightly brush a 600ml/1 pint/2½ cup loaf tin with oil. On a lightly floured surface, roll out the pastry until it is about 3mm/⅛in thick. Cut rectangles to fit the base and sides of the tin and press them in place. Press the edges together to seal them. Cut a piece of pastry to fit the top of the tin and set it aside.

4 Spoon half the chestnut mixture into the tin and level the surface. Sprinkle on a layer of the cranberries and cover with the remaining chestnut mixture. Cover the filling with the pastry lid and pinch the edges to join them to the sides. Dust the work surface with flour, then cut shapes from the pastry trimmings to use as decorations.

5 Brush the pastry top and the decorative shapes with the beaten egg glaze and arrange the shapes in a pattern on top.

6 Bake the loaf in the oven for about 35 minutes, or until the crust is golden brown. Decorate the top of the loaf with fresh cranberries. Serve hot.

Spiced Vegetable Couscous

Couscous, a cereal processed from semolina, is used throughout North Africa, mostly in Morocco.

It is traditionally served with Moroccan vegetable stews or tagines but makes a fabulous alternative

Christmas dish. You can serve it on its own or with roasted meat or poultry.

INGREDIENTS

45ml/3 tbsp vegetable oil
1 large onion, finely chopped
2 garlic cloves, crushed
15ml/1 tbsp tomato purée
2.5ml/½ tsp ground turmeric
2.5ml/½ tsp cayenne pepper
5ml/1 tsp each ground coriander and cumin
225g/8oz/1½ cups cauliflower florets
225g/8oz baby carrots
1 red (bell) pepper, seeded and diced
4 beefsteak tomatoes
225g/8oz/1¼ cups thickly sliced
courgettes (zucchini)
400g/14oz can chick-peas, drained
and rinsed
45ml/3 tbsp chopped fresh
coriander (cilantro)
salt and freshly ground black pepper
coriander (cilantro) sprigs, to garnish

For the Couscous
450g/1lb/2⅔ cups couscous
5ml/1 tsp salt
50g/2oz/2 tbsp butter

Serves 6

1 Heat 30ml/2 tbsp of the oil in a pan, add the onion and garlic, and cook until translucent. Stir in the tomato purée, turmeric, cayenne, ground coriander and cumin. Cook for 2 minutes.

2 Add the cauliflower, carrots and pepper, then pour in enough water to come just halfway up the vegetables. Bring to the boil, then lower the heat, cover and simmer gently for about 10 minutes.

3 Plunge the tomatoes into boiling water for 30 seconds, then refresh in cold water. When cool enough to handle, peel away the skins and chop. Add the sliced courgettes, chick-peas and tomatoes to the carrot, cauliflower and pepper mixture then cook for a further 10 minutes. Stir in the fresh coriander then season generously with salt and pepper. Set aside and keep hot until you have cooked the couscous and are ready to serve the meal.

4 To cook the couscous, bring 475ml/16fl oz/2 cups water to the boil in a large saucepan. Add the remaining oil and the salt. Remove from the heat, and add the couscous, stirring. Allow to swell for 2 minutes, then add the butter, and heat through gently, stirring to separate the grains.

5 Turn the couscous out on to a warm serving dish, and spoon the vegetables on top, pouring over any liquid. Garnish with the coriander sprigs and serve the couscous at once.

COOK'S TIP

Beefsteak tomatoes have excellent flavour and are ideal for this recipe, but you can substitute six ordinary tomatoes or two 400g/14oz cans chopped tomatoes, if beefsteak tomatoes are not available.

Filo Vegetable Pie

This stunning pie packed with winter vegetables and other goodies makes a delicious

main course for vegetarians. For meat-eaters, it is an excellent accompaniment to

cold sliced turkey or other meat dishes.

INGREDIENTS

225g/8oz leeks
165g/5½oz/11 tbsp butter
225g/8oz carrots, cubed
225g/8oz/3 cups sliced mushrooms
225g/8oz Brussels sprouts, quartered
2 garlic cloves, crushed
115g/4oz/½ cup cream cheese
115g/4oz/½ cup Roquefort or
Stilton cheese
150ml/¼ pint/⅔ cup double (heavy) cream
2 eggs, beaten
225g/8oz cooking apples
225g/8oz/1 cup cashew nuts or
pine nuts, toasted
350g/12oz frozen filo pastry, defrosted
salt and freshly ground black pepper

Serves 6–8

3 Whisk the cream cheese and blue cheese, cream, eggs and seasoning together in a bowl. Pour them over the vegetables. Peel and core the apples and cut into 1cm/½in cubes. Stir them into the vegetables. Lastly, add the toasted cashew or pine nuts.

5 Spoon in the vegetable mixture and fold over the excess filo pastry to cover the filling.

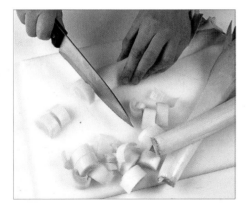

1 Preheat the oven to 180°C/350°F/ Gas 4. Cut the leeks in half lengthways and wash them, separating the layers slightly to check they are clean. Slice into 1cm/½in pieces, drain and dry.

2 Heat 40g/1½oz/3 tbsp of the butter in a large pan and cook the leeks and carrots covered over a medium heat for 5 minutes. Add the mushrooms, sprouts and garlic and cook for another 2 minutes. Turn the vegetables into a bowl and let them cool.

4 Melt the remaining butter. Brush all over the inside of a 23cm/9in loose-based springform cake tin with melted butter. Brush two-thirds of the filo pastry sheets with butter, one sheet at a time, and use them to line the base and sides of the tin, overlapping the layers so that there are no gaps for the filling to fall through.

6 Brush the remaining filo sheets with butter and cut them into 2.5cm/1in strips. Cover the top of the pie with these strips, arranging them in a rough mound. Bake for 35–45 minutes until golden brown. Stand for 5 minutes, then unclip the spring and remove the cake tin. Transfer the pie to a serving plate.

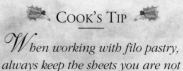
COOK'S TIP
When working with filo pastry, always keep the sheets you are not using under a clean, damp cloth to prevent them from drying out.

FESTIVE BRUSSELS SPROUTS

This classic dish is always a favourite at Christmas. Be sure to allow plenty of time to peel the

chestnuts; this is very time-consuming but well worth the effort.

INGREDIENTS

450g/1lb fresh chestnuts
450ml/¾ pint/1⅞ cups vegetable stock
450g/1lb Brussels sprouts
450g/1lb carrots
25g/1oz/2 tbsp butter
salt and freshly ground black pepper

Serves 8

1 Peel the raw chestnuts, leaving the brown papery skins intact. Drop them into boiling water for a few minutes, then remove will a slotted spoon. The skins should slip off easily.

2 Put the peeled chestnuts in a pan with the stock. Cover and bring to the boil. Simmer for 10 minutes. Drain.

3 Peel and trim the sprouts. Boil in salted water for 5 minutes. Drain.

4 Cut the carrots in 1cm/½in diagonal slices. Put them in a pan with cold water to cover, bring to the boil and simmer for about 6 minutes. Drain. Melt the butter in a clean pan, add the chestnuts, sprouts and carrots and season. Serve hot.

CREAMY SPINACH PURÉE

Crème fraîche, the thick French soured cream, or béchamel sauce usually gives this spinach recipe

its creamy texture, but try this quick, richly flavoured alternative.

INGREDIENTS

675g/1½lb leaf spinach, stems removed
115g/4oz/1 cup full- or
medium-fat soft cheese
milk (if needed)
freshly grated nutmeg
salt and freshly ground black pepper

Serves 4

1 Rinse the spinach thoroughly under running water to remove any grit. Shake lightly and place in a deep frying pan or wok with just the water clinging to the leaves. Cook, uncovered, over a medium heat for 3–4 minutes until wilted.

2 Drain the spinach in a colander or large sieve (strainer), pressing out the excess moisture with the back of a large spoon; the spinach doesn't need to be completely dry.

3 In a food processor fitted with a metal blade, purée the spinach and soft cheese, then transfer to a bowl. If the purée is too thick, add a little milk.

4 Season the spinach with salt, pepper and grated nutmeg. Transfer to a heavy pan and reheat gently. Place in a serving dish and serve hot.

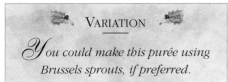
VARIATION

You could make this purée using Brussels sprouts, if preferred.

LEEK AND ONION TART

This simple recipe isn't a normal tart with pastry, but an all-in-one savoury slice

that is excellent served as an accompaniment to roast meat.

INGREDIENTS

50g/2oz/4 tbsp unsalted butter
350g/12oz leeks, sliced thinly
350g/12oz onions, sliced thinly
225g/8oz/2 cups self-raising
(self-rising) flour
115g/4oz/½ cup white cooking fat
150ml/¼ pint/⅔ cup water
salt and freshly ground black pepper

Serves 4

1 Preheat the oven to 200°C/400°F/Gas 6. Melt the butter in a pan and sauté the leeks and onions until soft. Season well with salt and black pepper.

2 Mix the flour, fat and water together in a large bowl to make a soft but sticky dough. Mix into the leek mixture in the pan. Place the contents of the pan in a greased shallow ovenproof dish and level the surface with a palette knife. Bake in the preheated oven for about 30 minutes, or until brown and crispy. Serve the tart sliced, as a vegetable side dish.

COOK'S TIP

Onions keep very well stored in a cool, dry place. Do not store them in the refrigerator as they will go soft, and never keep cut onions in the refrigerator unless you want onion-scented milk and an onion-scented home.

VARIATION

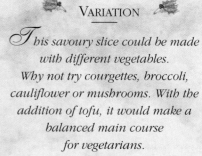

This savoury slice could be made with different vegetables. Why not try courgettes, broccoli, cauliflower or mushrooms. With the addition of tofu, it would make a balanced main course for vegetarians.

THYME-ROASTED ONIONS

These slow-roasted onions develop a delicious, sweet flavour that's the perfect accompaniment

to roast meat. You could prepare par-boiled new potatoes in the same way.

INGREDIENTS

75ml/5 tbsp olive oil
50g/2oz/4 tbsp unsalted butter
900g/2lb small onions
30ml/2 tbsp chopped fresh thyme
salt and freshly ground black pepper

Serves 4

1 Preheat the oven to 220°C/425°F/ Gas 7. Heat the oil and butter together in a large roasting tin. Remove the outer layer from the onions, otherwise keeping them whole.

2 Add the onions to the roasting tin and toss them in the oil and butter mixture over a medium heat until they are very lightly sautéed and just beginning to brown.

3 Add the thyme and seasoning and roast for 45 minutes, basting regularly.

COOK'S TIP

*B*aby yellow or vidalia onions would be perfect for use in this dish as both types are recommended for slow-roasting. Shallots could be used as a pleasant alternative, since they taste excellent cooked in this way.

Sweet and Sour Red Cabbage

This cabbage dish can be cooked the day before and reheated for serving. It is a good

accompaniment to goose, pork or strong-flavoured game dishes.

Ingredients

900g/2lb red cabbage
30ml/2 tbsp olive oil
2 large onions, sliced
2 large cooking apples, peeled, cored
and sliced
30ml/2 tbsp cider vinegar
30ml/2 tbsp soft light brown sugar
225g/8oz rindless streaky (fatty) bacon,
chopped (optional)
salt and freshly ground black pepper

Serves 8

1 Preheat the oven to 180°C/350°F/ Gas 4. Cut the cabbage into quarters and shred it finely with a sharp knife.

2 Heat the oil in a large ovenproof casserole. Cook the onion over a gentle heat for 2 minutes.

3 Stir the cabbage, apples, vinegar, sugar and seasoning into the casserole. Cover and cook for 1 hour, until tender. Stir halfway through cooking.

4 Fry the bacon, if using, until crisp. Stir it into the cabbage before serving.

PARSNIP AND CHESTNUT CROQUETTES

These tasty croquettes are a delightful way to present classic Christmas vegetables. They can

easily be made ahead of time and chilled until they are required.

INGREDIENTS

*450g/1lb parsnips, cut roughly into
small pieces
115g/4oz frozen chestnuts
25g/1oz/2 tbsp butter
1 garlic clove, crushed
15ml/1 tbsp chopped fresh
coriander (cilantro)
1 egg, beaten
40–50g/1½–2 oz/½ cup fresh white
breadcrumbs
vegetable oil, for frying
salt and freshly ground black pepper
sprig of coriander (cilantro), to garnish*

Makes 10–12

1 Place the parsnips in a saucepan with enough water to cover. Bring to the boil, cover and simmer for about 15–20 minutes, until tender.

2 Place the frozen chestnuts in a pan of water, bring to the boil and simmer gently for 8–10 minutes, until they are very tender. Drain, then place the chestnuts in a mixing bowl and mash roughly.

3 Melt the butter in a small saucepan and cook the garlic for 30 seconds. Drain the parsnips and mash, then mix with the garlic butter. Stir in the chestnuts and chopped coriander, then season well.

4 Take about 15ml/1 tbsp of the mixture at a time and form into croquettes, 7.5cm/3in long. Dip into the egg, then roll in breadcrumbs.

5 Heat a little oil in a frying pan and fry the croquettes for 3–4 minutes until golden, turning frequently so they brown evenly. Drain on kitchen paper and serve, garnished with coriander.

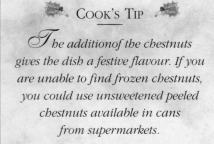

COOK'S TIP

The addition of the chestnuts gives the dish a festive flavour. If you are unable to find frozen chestnuts, you could use unsweetened peeled chestnuts available in cans from supermarkets.

Glazed Carrots with Cider

This recipe is extremely simple to make. The carrots are cooked in the minimum of liquid

to bring out the best of their flavour, and the cider adds a pleasant sharpness.

2 Melt the butter in a heavy-based frying pan, add the carrots and sauté for 4–5 minutes, stirring often. Sprinkle with the sugar and cook, stirring for 1 minute or until the sugar has dissolved.

3 Add the cider and stock or water to the frying pan. Bring to the boil and stir in the Dijon mustard. Partially cover the pan with the lid and simmer for about 10–12 minutes, until the carrots are just tender. Remove the lid and continue cooking until the liquid has reduced to a thick sauce.

4 Remove the sauce from the heat and stir in the chopped fresh parsley. Spoon the carrots into a warmed serving dish. Serve as an accompaniment to grilled meat or fish or with a vege-

INGREDIENTS

450g/1lb young carrots
25g/1oz/2 tbsp butter
15ml/1 tbsp soft light brown sugar
120ml/4fl oz/½ cup cider
60ml/4 tbsp vegetable stock or water
5ml/1 tsp Dijon mustard
15ml/1 tbsp finely chopped fresh parsley

Serves 4

1 Trim the tops and bottoms off all of the carrots. Peel or scrape them. Using a sharp knife, cut them into julienne strips.

COOK'S TIP

If the carrots are cooked before the liquid in the saucepan has reduced, transfer the carrots to a serving dish and rapidly boil the liquid until thick. Pour over the carrots and sprinkle with parsley.

STIR-FRIED BRUSSELS SPROUTS

Many people are wary of eating Brussels sprouts because they are often overcooked. This recipe

makes the most of the vegetable's flavour and has the added interest of an oriental twist.

INGREDIENTS

450g/1lb Brussels sprouts
15ml/1 tbsp sunflower oil
6–8 spring onions, cut into
2.5cm/1in lengths
2 slices fresh root ginger
40g/1½oz/⅓ cup slivered almonds
150–175ml/4–6fl oz/⅔– ¾ cup vegetable or
chicken stock
salt

Serves 4

1 Remove any large outer leaves and trim the bases of the Brussels sprouts. Cut into slices about 7mm/½in thick.

2 Heat the oil in a wok or large heavy-based frying pan, and fry the spring onions and the fresh root ginger for 2–3 minutes, stirring frequently. Add the almonds and stir-fry over a moderate heat until both the onions and almonds just begin to brown.

3 Remove and discard the ginger, reduce the heat and stir in the Brussels sprouts. Stir-fry for a few minutes and then pour in the vegetable or chicken stock and cook, stirring, over a gentle heat for 5–6 minutes, or until the sprouts are nearly tender.

4 Add a little salt to the wok or frying pan, if necessary, and then increase the heat to boil off all the excess liquid. Check they are tender then spoon the Brussels sprouts into a warmed serving dish and serve immediately.

> ### COOK'S TIP
>
> *If you want to further enhance the oriental flavour of this dish, you could add a couple of dashes of light soy sauce and a sprinkling of sesame oil.*

Peas with Baby Onions and Cream

Ideally, use fresh peas and fresh baby onions for this dish. Frozen peas

can be used if fresh ones aren't available, but frozen onions tend to be insipid

and are not worth using. Alternatively, you could use the white part of spring onions.

INGREDIENTS

175g/6oz baby onions
15g/½oz/1 tbsp butter
900g/2lb fresh peas or 350g/12oz/
3 cups shelled or frozen peas
150ml/¼ pint/⅔ cup double (heavy) cream
15g/½oz/1 tbsp plain (all-purpose) flour
10ml/2 tsp chopped fresh parsley
15–30ml/1–2 tbsp lemon juice (optional)
salt and freshly ground black pepper

Serves 4

1 Remove the outer layer of skin from the onions and then halve them, if necessary. Melt the butter in a flameproof casserole and fry the onions for 5–6 minutes over a medium heat, until they are just beginning to brown and are tender.

2 Add the peas and stir-fry for a few minutes. Add 120ml/4fl oz/½ cup water and bring to the boil. Simmer for about 10 minutes until both are tender. There should be a thin layer of water on the base of the pan.

3 Blend the cream with the flour. Remove the frying pan from the heat and stir in the cream, flour and fresh parsley and season to taste.

4 Cook over a gentle heat for about 3–4 minutes, until the sauce is thick. Add a little lemon juice, if using.

French Beans with Bacon and Cream

This baked vegetable accompaniment is rich and full of flavour. It is particularly good

with many poultry dishes, such as chicken or guinea fowl, and would be equally

tasty made with vegetarian bacon.

Ingredients

350g/12oz French beans
50–75g/2–3oz bacon, chopped
25g/1oz/2 tbsp butter or margarine
15ml/1 tbsp plain (all-purpose) flour
350ml/12fl oz/1½ cups milk and single
(light) cream, mixed
salt and freshly ground black pepper

Serves 4

1 Preheat the oven to 190°C/375°F/ Gas 5. Trim the beans and cook in lightly salted boiling water for about 5 minutes or until they are just tender. Drain and place them in an ovenproof dish.

2 Dry fry the chopped bacon until it is crisp, stirring it constantly to make sure that it doesn't stick to the frying pan. Crumble the bacon into very small pieces, then add to the oven-proof dish. Stir to mix with the beans then set aside.

3 Melt the butter or margarine in a large saucepan, stir in the flour and then add the milk and cream to make a smooth sauce, stirring continuously. Season well with plenty of salt and freshly ground black pepper.

4 Add the sauce to the beans and bacon and mix. Cover with foil and bake for 15–20 minutes. Serve.

Sautéed Potatoes

These rosemary-scented, crisp golden potatoes are an extra-special treat at Christmas time. If you use butter, keep a careful eye on the potatoes and check that they are not burning. A mixture of oil and butter would work well, giving a golden brown colour without catching and burning.

INGREDIENTS

*1.5kg/3lb baking potatoes
60–90ml/4–6 tbsp oil, bacon dripping or clarified butter
2 or 3 fresh rosemary sprigs, leaves removed and chopped
salt and freshly ground black pepper*

Serves 6

1 Peel the potatoes and cut into 2.5cm/1in pieces. Place them in a bowl, cover with cold water and leave to soak for 10–15 minutes. Drain, rinse and drain, then dry in a tea towel.

2 In a large, heavy non-stick frying pan or wok, heat about 60ml/4 tbsp of the oil, dripping or butter over a medium-high heat, until very hot, but not smoking.

COOK'S TIP

Soaking the potatoes before cooking removes excess starch, and patting them dry before cooking results in a crispier coating to the cooked potatoes.

3 Add the potatoes to the frying pan and cook for 2 minutes, without stirring, so that they seal completely and brown on one side.

4 Shake the pan and toss the potatoes to brown them on the other side, and continue to stir and shake the pan until the potatoes are evenly browned all over. Season with salt and pepper.

5 Add a little more oil, dripping or butter to the frying pan and continue cooking the potatoes over a medium-low to low heat for 20–25 minutes, until tender when pierced with a knife. Stir and shake the pan frequently. About 5 minutes before the end of cooking, sprinkle the potatoes with the chopped fresh rosemary sprigs.

HASSELBACK POTATOES

This is an unusual version of the famous Swedish recipe. Virtually any topping can be used; in this Yuletide

variation, the crispy potatoes are roasted in oil and butter, then coated in an orange glaze and

returned to the oven until deep golden brown and crunchy.

INGREDIENTS

4 large potatoes
25g/1oz/2 tbsp butter, melted
45ml/3 tbsp olive oil

For the Glaze
juice of 1 orange
grated rind of ½ orange
15ml/1 tbsp demerara sugar
freshly ground black pepper

Serves 4–6

1 Preheat the oven to 190°C/375°F/ Gas 5. Cut each potato in half lengthways. To score the potatoes for decoration, place them flat-side down on the chopping board and then cut down as if making very thin slices, but leaving the bottom 1cm/½in intact.

2 Place the potatoes in a large roasting dish. Using a pastry brush, coat the potatoes generously with the melted butter and pour the olive oil over the base and around the potatoes.

3 Bake the potatoes in the preheated oven for 40–50 minutes, just until they begin to turn brown.

4 Meanwhile, place the orange juice, orange rind and sugar in a small saucepan and heat gently, stirring until the sugar has dissolved. Simmer for 3–4 minutes, until the glaze is fairly thick, and then remove from the heat.

5 When the potatoes begin to brown, brush all over with the orange glaze and return to the oven to roast for a further 15 minutes or until the potatoes are a deep golden brown. Transfer to a warmed serving plate and serve.

Party Foods and Buffet Dishes

*G*one are the days of an uninspiring bowl of peanuts or

a mediocre choice of cheeses and canapés. The tremendous

range of ingredients available in the shops today means

that there are endless possibilities for lavish festive party

foods. Try mixing a few of these fabulous dishes for a truly

international taste – include Tapas of Almonds, Olives and

Cheese, or Blinis with Smoked Salmon and Dill Cream.

For vegetarians, try Mini Filled Jacket Potatoes or Mini Leek and

Onion Tartlets. Spoil your guests with sweet Filo Crackers with

Lemon Sauce, or provide a more substantial dish such

as a Turkey and Cranberry Pie and help them celebrate

the festive season in style.

CHEESELETS

These crispy cheese biscuits are irresistible, and will disappear in moments. They are very quick

and simple to make and you can use different cheeses to add variety.

2 Divide the mixture in half, add the Cheddar to one half and the Gruyère to the other. Using a fork or your fingertips, work each mixture into a soft dough and knead on a floured surface until smooth.

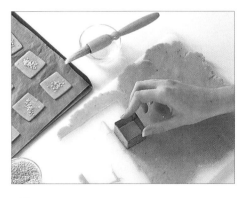

3 Roll out both pieces of dough very thinly and cut into 2.5cm/1in squares. Transfer to the lined baking sheets. Brush the squares with beaten egg white, sprinkle with sesame seeds and bake for 5–6 minutes or until slightly puffed up and pale gold in colour.

4 Cool the cheeselets on the baking sheets, then carefully remove with a palette knife. Repeat the process until you have used up all the biscuit dough.

5 Pack the biscuits in airtight tins or present as a gift, packed in attractively decorated boxes tied with ribbon or in glass bowls.

INGREDIENTS

115g/4oz/1 cup plain (all-purpose) flour
2.5ml/½tsp salt
2.5ml/½ tsp cayenne pepper
2.5ml/1½ tsp dry mustard
115g/4oz/½ cup butter
50g/2oz/½ cup grated Cheddar cheese
50g/2oz/½ cup grated Gruyère cheese
1 egg white, beaten
15g/1 tbsp sesame seeds

Makes about 80

1 Preheat the oven to 220°C/425°F/ Gas 7. Line several baking sheets with non-stick baking paper. Sift the flour, salt, cayenne pepper and mustard into a mixing bowl. Cut the butter into pieces and rub into the flour mixture.

Cocktail Biscuits

Tiny savoury biscuits are always a welcome treat. Experiment with different flavours and

shapes, and make a batch of biscuits to give as gifts.

Ingredients

350g/12oz/3 cups plain (all-purpose) flour
2.5ml/½ tsp salt
2.5ml/½ tsp black pepper
5ml/1 tsp wholegrain mustard
175g/6oz/¾ cup butter
115g/4oz/½ cup grated Cheddar
1 egg, beaten

Flavourings

5ml/1 tsp chopped nuts
10ml/2 tsp dill seeds
10ml/2 tsp curry paste
10ml/2 tsp chilli sauce

Makes about 80

2 Knead chopped nuts into one piece, dill seeds into another piece and curry paste and chilli sauce into each of the remaining pieces. Wrap each piece of flavoured dough in clear film and leave to chill in the refrigerator for at least an hour. Remove from the clear film and roll out one piece at a time.

3 Using different shaped cutters, stamp out about 20 shapes from each piece. Arrange the shapes on the baking sheets and bake in the oven for 6–8 minutes or until slightly puffed up and pale gold in colour. Cool on wire racks, then remove the biscuits from the baking sheets, using a palette knife.

1 Preheat the oven to 200°C/400°F/ Gas 6. Line several baking sheets with non-stick baking paper. Sift the flour into a mixing bowl and add the salt, pepper and mustard. Cut the butter into pieces and rub into the flour mixture until it resembles fine breadcrumbs. Use a fork to stir in the cheese and egg, and mix together to form a soft dough. Knead lightly on a floured surface and cut into 4 equal pieces.

71

TAPAS OF ALMONDS, OLIVES AND CHEESE

These three simple ingredients are lightly flavoured to create a delicious Spanish tapas medley

that is perfect for a casual starter or nibbles to serve with pre-dinner drinks.

INGREDIENTS

2.5ml/½ tsp coriander seeds
2.5ml/½ tsp fennel seeds
5ml/1 tsp chopped fresh rosemary
10ml/2 tsp chopped fresh parsley
2 garlic cloves, crushed
15ml/1 tbsp sherry vinegar
30ml/2 tbsp olive oil
115g/4oz/⅔ cup black olives
115g/4oz/⅔ cup green olives

For the Marinated Cheese
150g/5oz goat's cheese
90ml/6 tbsp olive oil
15ml/1 tbsp white wine vinegar
5ml/1 tsp black peppercorns
1 garlic clove, sliced
3 fresh tarragon or thyme sprigs
tarragon sprigs, to garnish

For the Salted Almonds
1.5ml/¼ tsp cayenne pepper
30ml/2 tbsp sea salt
25g/1oz/2 tbsp butter
60ml/4 tbsp olive oil
200g/7oz/1¾ cups blanched almonds
extra sea salt for sprinkling (optional)

Serves 6–8

🌿 COOK'S TIP 🌿

If serving with pre-dinner drinks, provide cocktail sticks for spearing the olives and cheese.

1 To make the marinated olives, crush the coriander and fennel seeds with a pestle and mortar. Or, put them into a strong plastic bag and crush them with a rolling pin.

2 Mix the olives and seeds with the rosemary, parsley, garlic, vinegar and oil and pour over the olives in a small bowl. Cover with clear film and chill for up to 1 week.

3 To make the marinated cheese, cut the goat's cheese into bitesize pieces, leaving the rind on. Mix together the oil, vinegar, peppercorns, garlic and herb sprigs and pour over the cheese in a small bowl. Cover with clear film and chill for up to 3 days.

4 To make the salted almonds, mix together the cayenne pepper and salt in a large mixing bowl. Melt the butter with the olive oil in a frying pan. Add the almonds to the frying pan and stir-fry for about 5 minutes, until the almonds are golden.

5 Tip the almonds out of the frying pan, into the salt mixture, and toss together until the almonds are coated. Leave to cool, then remove with a slotted spoon and store them in a jar or airtight container for up to 1 week.

6 To serve the tapas, arrange in small, shallow serving dishes. Use fresh sprigs of tarragon to garnish the cheese and scatter the almonds with a little more salt, if desired.

BLINIS WITH SMOKED SALMON AND DILL CREAM

This recipe is perfect for any festive celebration. Your guests will appreciate fresh, authentic home-made blinis and will enjoy them with a glass of sparkling wine. Instead of salmon, you could top the blinis with caviar or the less expensive lumpfish caviar.

INGREDIENTS

115g/4oz/scant cup buckwheat flour
115g/4oz/1 cup plain (all-purpose) flour
pinch of salt
15ml/1 tbsp easy-blend (rapid rise) dried yeast
2 eggs
350ml/12fl oz/1½ cups warm milk
15g/½oz/1 tbsp melted butter,
150ml/¼ pint/⅔ cup crème fraîche
45ml/3 tbsp chopped fresh dill
225g/8oz smoked salmon, thinly sliced
fresh dill sprigs, to garnish

4 Whisk the remaining egg white until it holds stiff peaks, then, using a metal spoon, fold into the batter.

5 Preheat a heavy-based frying pan or griddle and brush with melted butter. Drop tablespoons of the batter on to the pan, spacing them well apart. Cook for about 40 seconds, until bubbles appear on the surface.

6 Flip over the blinis and cook for 30 seconds on the other side. Wrap in foil and keep warm in a low oven. Repeat with the remaining mixture, buttering the pan each time.

7 Combine the crème fraîche and dill. Serve the blinis topped with the smoked salmon and dill cream. Garnish each with dill sprigs. Serve.

1 Mix the flours in a large bowl with salt. Sprinkle in the yeast, and mix.

2 Separate one egg. Whisk together the whole egg and the yolk, the warmed milk and the melted butter.

3 Pour on to the flour mixture. Beat to form a smooth batter. Cover with clear film and leave to rise for 1–2 hours.

Mini Filled Jacket Potatoes

Jacket potatoes are always delicious, and the toppings can easily be varied: choose from luxurious

and extravagant ingredients, such as caviar and smoked salmon, to equally satisfying,

but more everyday fare, such as cheese and baked beans.

INGREDIENTS

36 potatoes, well scrubbed
250ml/8fl oz/1 cup thick soured
(sour) cream
45–60ml/3–4 tbsp snipped fresh chives
coarse salt, for sprinkling

Makes 36

COOK'S TIP

The potatoes can be baked in advance in the oven, then reheated in the microwave on high (100%) for 3–4 minutes.

1 Preheat the oven to 180°C/350°F/ Gas 4. Place the potatoes on a baking sheet and bake in the oven for 30–35 minutes, or until the potatoes are tender when pierced with the tip of a sharp kitchen knife.

2 To serve, make a cross in the top of each potato and squeeze very gently to open. Make a hollow in the centre of each potato. Fill each one with soured cream, then sprinkle with the salt and the snipped chives. Serve immediately.

VARIATION

If your guests are likely to be hungry, use medium-size potatoes. When cooked, cut in half, scoop out the flesh, mash with the other ingredients and spoon the mixture back into the skin. Serve warm.

Filo Crackers with Lemon Sauce

These festive-shaped sweet treats will make any party go with a bang! The crackers can be

prepared a day in advance, brushed with melted butter and kept covered with clear film

in the refrigerator or freezer before baking.

INGREDIENTS

*2 x 275g/10oz packet frozen filo
pastry, thawed
115g/4oz/½ cup butter, melted
thin foil ribbon, to decorate
sifted icing (confectioner's) sugar,
to decorate*

For the Filling
*450g/1lb eating apples, peeled, cored and
finely chopped
5ml/1 tsp ground cinnamon
25g/1oz/2 tbsp soft light brown sugar
50g/2oz/½ cup chopped pecan nuts
50g/2oz/1 cup fresh white breadcrumbs
25g/1oz/3 tbsp sultanas (golden raisins)
25g/1oz/3 heaped tbsp currants*

For the Lemon Sauce
*115g/4oz/⅔ cup caster (superfine) sugar
finely grated rind of 1 lemon
juice of 2 lemons*

Makes about 24

1 Unwrap the filo pastry and cover it with clear film (plastic wrap) and a damp cloth, to prevent it from drying out. Put the chopped apples in a large bowl and mix in the remaining filling ingredients.

2 Take one sheet of pastry at a time and cut it into 15 x 30cm/6 x 12in strips. Brush with butter. Place a spoonful of the filling at one end and fold in the sides, so the pastry measures 13cm/5in across. Brush the edges with the melted butter and roll up. Pinch the "frill" tightly at either end of the cracker. Brush once again with melted butter.

3 Place the crackers on baking trays, cover and chill for 10 minutes. Preheat the oven to 190°C/375°F/Gas 5. Brush each cracker with melted butter. Bake the crackers for 30–35 minutes, or until they are golden brown. Let them cool slightly on the baking trays and then transfer them to a wire rack to allow them to cool completely.

4 To make the lemon sauce, put all the ingredients in a small saucepan and heat gently until all of the ingredients are dissolved, stirring occasionally. Pour the warm sauce into a sauce boat and serve with the filo crackers.

COOK'S TIP
Make sure people know they will be eating a sweet-filled cracker by dredging the serving plate with icing sugar.

VARIATION
If you have any leftover mincemeat, you could use it as an alternative filling and serve both varieties together.

Game Terrine

This country terrine should be made with the best meat your butcher has to offer. It is delicious

served as an appetizer or with salads and other cold meats as part of a buffet spread.

INGREDIENTS

225g/8oz rindless, unsmoked streaky
(fatty) bacon rashers (strips)
225g/8oz lamb's or pig's liver, minced
450g/1lb minced (ground) pork
1 small onion, finely chopped
2 garlic, cloves, crushed
10ml/2 tsp mixed dried herbs
225g/8oz game of your choice
60ml/4 tbsp port or sherry
1 bay leaf
50g/2oz/4 tbsp plain (all-purpose) flour
300ml/½ pint/1¼ cups aspic jelly, made up
as packet instructions
salt and freshly ground black pepper

Serves 8

2 Mix the minced meats with the chopped onion, garlic and mixed dried herbs. Season well with plenty of salt and ground black pepper.

5 Preheat the oven to 160°C/325°F/ Gas 3. Put the flour into a small bowl and mix it to a firm dough with 30–45ml/2–3 tbsp cold water. Cover the terrine with a lid and seal it with the flour paste. Place the terrine in a roasting tin and pour around enough hot water to come halfway up the sides of the tin. Cook in the preheated oven for about 2 hours.

1 Remove the rind from the bacon and stretch each rasher with the back of a heavy kitchen knife. Use the bacon to line a 1 litre/1¾ pint/4 cup terrine. The terrine should be ovenproof and must have a lid to seal in all the flavours during the long cooking time.

3 Use a heavy kitchen knife to cut the game into thin strips, and put the meat into a large mixing bowl with the port or sherry. Season the game.

4 Put one-third of the minced mixture into the terrine. Press the mixture well into the corners. Cover with half the strips of game and repeat these layers, ending with a minced layer. Level the surface and lay the bay leaf on top.

6 Remove the lid and weight the terrine down with a 2kg/4lb weight. Leave to cool. Remove any fat from the surface and cover with warmed aspic jelly. Chill overnight before turning out on to a serving plate. Serve the terrine cut into thin slices with a mixed salad and some fruit-based chutney.

COOK'S TIP

You can use hare, rabbit, pheasant or pigeon for this dish.

FILLET OF BEEF WITH RATATOUILLE

This succulent rare beef is served cold with a colourful garlicky ratatouille.

INGREDIENTS

700–900g/1½–2lb fillet of beef
45ml/3 tbsp olive oil
300ml/½ pint/1¼ cups aspic jelly, made up
as packet instructions

For the Marinade
30ml/2 tbsp sherry
30ml/2 tbsp olive oil
30ml/2 tbsp soy sauce
10ml/2 tsp grated fresh root ginger or
5ml/1 tsp ground ginger
2 garlic cloves, crushed

For the Ratatouille
60ml/4 tbsp olive oil
1 onion, sliced
2–3 garlic cloves, crushed
1 large aubergine (eggplant), cubed
1 each small red, green and yellow (bell)
pepper, seeded and sliced
225g/8oz courgettes (zucchini), sliced
450g/1lb tomatoes, skinned and quartered
15ml/1 tbsp chopped mixed fresh herbs
30ml/2 tbsp French dressing
salt and freshly ground black pepper

Serves 8

1 Mix all the marinade ingredients together in a shallow dish, put the beef in and turn it over to coat it. Cover the dish with clear film and leave for 30 minutes, to allow the flavours to penetrate.

2 Preheat the oven to 220°C/425°F/ Gas 7. Using a large slotted spoon, lift the fillet out of the marinade and pat it dry with kitchen paper. Heat the oil in a frying pan until smoking hot and then brown the beef all over to seal it. Transfer to a roasting tin and roast for 10–15 minutes, basting it occasionally with the marinade. Lift the beef on to a large plate and leave it to cool.

3 Meanwhile, for the ratatouille, heat the oil in a large casserole and cook the onion and garlic over a low heat, until tender, without letting the onions become brown. Add the aubergine cubes to the casserole and cook for a further 5 minutes, until soft. Add the sliced peppers and courgettes and cook for 2 minutes more. Then add the tomatoes, chopped herbs and season well with salt and pepper. Cook for a few minutes longer.

4 Turn the ratatouille into a dish and set aside to cool. Drizzle the ratatouille with a little French dressing. Cut the beef into slices and overlap them on a serving platter. Brush the slices with cold aspic jelly that is on the point of setting.

5 Leave the jelly to set completely, then brush with a second coat. Spoon the ratatouille around the beef and serve.

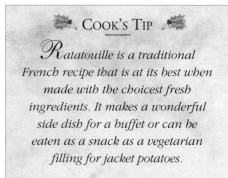

COOK'S TIP

Ratatouille is a traditional French recipe that is at its best when made with the choicest fresh ingredients. It makes a wonderful side dish for a buffet or can be eaten as a snack as a vegetarian filling for jacket potatoes.

TURKEY AND CRANBERRY PIE

The cranberries add a tart layer to this turkey pie. Cranberry sauce can be used

if fresh cranberries are not available. The pie freezes well and is an ideal dish to prepare in advance.

INGREDIENTS

450g/1lb pork sausage meat
(bulk sausage)
450g/1lb lean minced (ground) pork
15ml/1 tbsp ground coriander
15ml/1 tbsp mixed dried herbs
finely grated rind of 2 large oranges
10ml/2 tsp grated fresh root ginger or
2.5ml/½ tsp ground ginger
450g/1 lb turkey breast fillets, thinly sliced
115g/4oz/1 cup fresh cranberries
salt and freshly ground black pepper

For the Pastry
450g/1lb/4 cups plain (all-purpose) flour
5ml/1 tsp salt
150g/5oz/⅔ cup lard
150ml/¼ pint/⅔ cup mixed milk and water

To Finish
1 egg, beaten
300ml/½ pint/1¼ cups aspic jelly, made up
as packet instructions

Serves 8

1 Preheat the oven to 180°C/350°F/
Gas 4. Place a large baking tray in the
oven to preheat. In a large bowl, mix
together the sausagemeat, minced pork,
coriander, mixed dried herbs, orange
rind and ginger with plenty of salt and
freshly ground black pepper.

2 To make the pastry, put the flour into
a large bowl with the salt. Heat the lard
in a small pan with the milk and water
until just beginning to boil. Draw the
pan aside and allow to cool slightly.

3 Using a wooden spoon, quickly stir
the liquid into the flour until a very
stiff dough is formed. Turn on to a
work surface and knead until smooth.
Cut one-third off the dough for the
lid, wrap it in clear film and keep it
in a warm place.

4 Roll out the large piece of dough
on a floured surface and line the base
and sides of a well-greased 20cm/8in
loose-based, springform cake tin.
Work with the dough while it is still
warm, as it will start to crack and
break if it is left to get cold.

5 Put the turkey breast fillets between
two pieces of clear film and flatten with
a rolling pin to a 3mm/⅛in thickness.
Spoon half the pork mixture into the
base of the tin, pressing it well into the
edges. Cover with half of the turkey
slices and then the cranberries, followed
by the remaining turkey and finally the
rest of the pork mixture.

6 Roll out the rest of the dough and
cover the filling, trimming any excess
and sealing the edges with beaten egg.
Make a steam hole in the lid and
decorate with pastry trimmings.
Brush with beaten egg. Bake for
2 hours. Cover the pie with foil if it
gets too brown. Place the pie on a wire
rack to cool. When cold, use a funnel to
fill the pie with aspic jelly. Allow to set
overnight before unmoulding the pie.

Turkey Rice Salad

A delicious, crunchy salad to use up leftover turkey will be a welcome, refreshing change from

richer meals during the holiday festivities.

INGREDIENTS

225g/8oz/1¼ cups brown rice
50g/2oz/⅔ cup wild rice
2 red dessert apples, quartered,
cored and chopped
2 celery sticks, coarsely sliced
115g/4oz seedless grapes
45ml/3 tbsp lemon or orange juice
150ml/¼ pint/⅔ cup thick mayonnaise
350g/12oz cooked turkey, chopped
salt and freshly ground
black pepper
frilly lettuce leaves, to serve

Serves 8

1 Cook the brown and wild rice in boiling salted water for 25 minutes or until tender. Rinse under cold running water and drain.

2 Transfer the rice to a bowl, add the apples, celery and grapes. Mix the lemon or orange juice with the mayonnaise. Season and add to the rice.

3 Add the turkey and mix well to coat with the lemon or orange mayonnaise.

4 Line a warmed serving dish with the lettuce, and spoon the rice on top. Serve.

Chicken Roll

This roll can be prepared and cooked the day before it is needed and will freeze well, too.

Remove from the refrigerator about an hour before serving.

INGREDIENTS

2 kg/4lb chicken

For the Stuffing
1 medium onion, finely chopped
50g/2oz/4 tbsp melted butter
350g/12oz lean minced (ground) pork
115g/4oz streaky (fatty) bacon, chopped
15ml/1 tbsp chopped fresh parsley
10ml/2 tsp chopped fresh thyme
115g/4oz/2 cups fresh white breadcrumbs
30ml/2 tbsp sherry
1 large egg, beaten
25g/1oz/¼ cup shelled
pistachio nuts
25g/1oz/¼ cup stoned (pitted) black olives
(about 12)
salt and freshly ground black pepper

Serves 8

1 To make the stuffing, cook the chopped onion gently in a frying pan with 25g/1oz/2 tbsp butter until soft. Turn into a bowl and allow to cool. Add the remaining ingredients, mix thoroughly and season well with salt and freshly ground black pepper.

2 Place the chicken on a clean chopping board and bone it. To start, use a small, sharp knife to remove the wing tips. Turn the chicken over on to its breast and cut a deep line down the backbone.

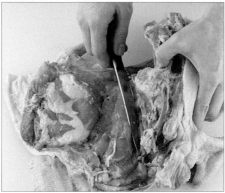

3 Cut the flesh away from the carcass, scraping the bones clean. Carefully cut through the sinew around the leg and wing joints and scrape down the bones to free them. Remove the carcass, taking care not to cut through the skin along the breastbone so that the stuffing will not escape during cooking.

4 To stuff the chicken, lay it flat, skin side down, and level the flesh as much as possible. Shape the stuffing down the centre and fold the sides over.

5 Sew the flesh together, using dark thread (this will be easier to see when the roll is cooked). Tie the flesh with string to form a roll.

6 Preheat the oven to 180°C/350°F/ Gas 4. Place the roll, with the join underneath, on a roasting rack in a roasting tin and brush with the remaining butter. Bake uncovered for about 1¼ hours or until cooked. Baste the chicken often. Leave to cool completely before removing the string and thread. Wrap in foil and chill until ready for serving or freezing.

CLASSIC WHOLE SALMON

Serving a boneless whole salmon is a delight. If you own a fish kettle the method is slightly different:

cover the salmon with water and a dash of white wine, add a bay leaf, sliced lemon and black

peppercorns, and bring to the boil for 6 minutes. Leave to cool completely in the water until cold.

Drain, pat dry, and continue as instructed in the recipe.

INGREDIENTS

1 whole salmon
3 bay leaves
1 lemon, sliced
12 black peppercorns
300ml/½ pint/1¼ cups water
150ml/¼ pint/⅔ cup white wine
2 cucumbers, thinly sliced
large bunches of mixed fresh herbs such
as parsley, chervil and chives, to
garnish
mayonnaise, to serve

Serves 8

1 Preheat the oven to 180°C/350°F/ Gas 4. Clean the inside of the salmon. Make sure all the gut has been removed and the inside cavity has been well rinsed in several changes of cold water and then wiped out with kitchen paper. Cut the tail into a neat "V" shape with a sharp pair of kitchen scissors. Place the fish on a large piece of double thickness foil. Lay the bay leaves, sliced lemon and black peppercorns inside the cavity. Wrap the foil around the fish and up the sides, and pour on the water and wine. Seal the parcel tightly and place in a large roasting tin.

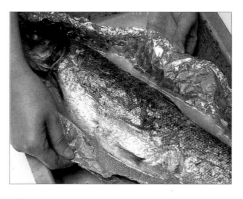

2 Bake in the preheated oven, allowing 15 minutes per pound plus 15 minutes extra. Remove from the oven, and, being careful not to scald yourself on the steam, open up the parcel. Leave to cool. Don't be tempted to leave the salmon to chill overnight because the skin will stick to the flesh and it will be impossible to remove the next day.

3 Using a sharp knife or a sharp pair of kitchen scissors, cut off the head and tail, reserving them if you want to display the fish later. Turn the fish upside-down on to a board so the flattest side is uppermost. Carefully peel off the base foil and the skin. Using a sharp knife, gently scrape away any excess brown flesh from the pink salmon flesh.

4 Make an incision down the back fillet, drawing the flesh away from the central bone. Take one fillet and place on the serving dish. Remove the second fillet and place it beside the first to form the base of the fish.

5 Carefully remove the central backbone from the salmon. Place the other half of the fish with the skin still intact, flesh-side down, on top of base fish. Peel off the upper skin and any brown bits. Replace the head and tail if required.

6 Lay the cucumber on top of the fish, working from the tail end until all the flesh is covered and the cucumber resembles scales. Garnish the serving plate with the fresh herbs of your choice. Serve with mayonnaise.

LAYERED SALMON TERRINE

This elegant fish mousse tastes as impressive as it looks. It would make a delicious appetizer,

or would be a perfect centrepiece for a Christmas buffet table.

INGREDIENTS

200ml/7fl oz/⅞ cup milk
50g/2oz/4 tbsp butter
65g/2½oz/⅔ cup plain (all-purpose) flour
450g/1lb fresh haddock fillet, boned and skinned
450g/1lb fresh salmon fillet, boned and skinned
2 eggs, beaten
60ml/4 tbsp double (heavy) cream
115g/4oz smoked salmon or trout, cut in strips
salt and freshly ground black pepper

Serves 8

2 Put the haddock into a blender and process it until smooth. Transfer to a bowl. Process the salmon fillet in the same way and put it into a separate bowl. Add an egg and half the cream to each mixture. Then beat in half the milk and flour paste to each mixture.

4 Spoon the haddock mixture into the tin and level the surface. Cover with the salmon mixture and level the surface.

1 Heat the milk and butter in a saucepan until the milk is boiling. Draw the saucepan aside and beat in the flour until a thick, smooth paste forms. Season well with salt and freshly ground black pepper, and turn the flour paste out on to a plate and leave to cool.

3 Preheat the oven to 180°C/350°F/ Gas 4. Butter a 900g/2lb loaf tin and line it with a piece of greaseproof paper. Lay strips of smoked salmon or trout diagonally over the base and up the side of the lined tin.

5 Cover with a layer of foil. Place it in a roasting tin and half fill the tin with hot water. Cook for 40 minutes.

VARIATIONS

Fresh trout fillets could be used instead of the salmon, and plaice fillets would make a good substitute for the haddock.

6 Remove from the oven and leave for 10 minutes. Turn the terrine out and serve it warm or cool.

Mini Leek and Onion Tartlets

The savoury filling in these tartlets is traditional to France where many types of quiche are popular.

Baking in individual tins makes for easier serving and looks attractive on the buffet table.

INGREDIENTS

25g/1oz/2 tbsp butter, cut into 8 pieces
1 onion, thinly sliced
2.5ml/½ tsp dried thyme
450g/1lb leeks, thinly sliced
*50g/2oz/5 tbsp grated Gruyère or
Emmenthal cheese*
3 eggs
300ml/½ pint/1¼ cups single (light) cream
pinch of freshly grated nutmeg
salt and freshly ground black pepper
*lettuce leaves, parsley leaves
and cherry
tomatoes, to serve*

For the Pastry
175g/6oz/1⅓ cup plain (all-purpose) flour
85g/3oz/6 tbsp cold butter
1 egg yolk
30–45ml/2–3 tbsp cold water
2.5ml/½ tsp salt

Serves 6

1 To make the pastry, sift the flour into a bowl and add the butter. Using your fingertips or a pastry blender, rub or cut the butter into the flour until the mixture resembles fine breadcrumbs.

2 Make a well in the flour mixture. In a small bowl, beat together the egg yolk, water and salt. Pour into the well and, using a fork, lightly combine the flour and liquid until the dough begins to stick together. Form into a flattened ball. Wrap and chill for 30 minutes.

3 Lightly butter six 10cm/4in tartlet tins. On a lightly floured surface, roll out the dough until about 3mm/⅛in thick, then using a 13cm/5in fluted cutter, cut out as many rounds as possible. Gently ease the pastry rounds firmly into the base and sides of each tin. Re-roll the trimmings and use to line the remaining tins. Prick the bases all over with a fork and chill for about 30 minutes.

4 Preheat the oven to 190°C/375°F/Gas 5. Line the pastry cases with foil and fill each one with baking beans or a large handful of dried pulses. Place them on a baking sheet and bake for 6–8 minutes until the pastry edges are golden. Lift out the foil and beans and bake the pastry cases for a further 2 minutes until the bases appear dry. Transfer to a wire rack and leave to cool. Reduce the oven temperature to 180°C/350°F/Gas 4.

5 In a large frying pan, melt the butter over a medium heat, then add the onion and thyme and cook for 3–5 minutes until the onion is just softened, stirring frequently. Add the leeks and cook for 10–12 minutes more until they are soft and tender. Divide the mixture among the cooled pastry cases and sprinkle each with cheese.

6 In a medium-size bowl, beat together the eggs, cream, nutmeg and salt and pepper. Place the pastry cases on a baking sheet and slowly pour in the egg mixture, being careful not to let them overflow.

7 Bake the tartlets for 15–20 minutes until they are set and golden. Transfer the tartlets to a wire rack to cool slightly, then remove them from the tins and serve while they are still warm, or at room temperature, with a mixture of lettuce and parsley leaves and cherry tomatoes.

Garden Vegetable Terrine

Perfect for a Christmas buffet menu, this is a softly set, creamy terrine of colourful vegetables

wrapped in glossy spinach leaves. Select large spinach leaves for the best results.

INGREDIENTS

225g/8oz fresh leaf spinach
3 carrots, cut in sticks
3–4 long, thin leeks
about 115g/4oz long green beans, topped and tailed
1 red (bell) pepper, cut in strips
2 courgettes (zucchini), cut in sticks
115g/4oz broccoli florets

For the Sauce
1 egg and 2 yolks
300ml/½ pint/1¼ cups single (light) cream
fresh nutmeg, grated
5ml/1 tsp salt
50g/2oz/½ cup grated Cheddar cheese
oil, for greasing
freshly ground black pepper

Serves 6

1 Preheat oven to 180°C/350°F/Gas 4. Blanch the spinach quickly in boiling water, then drain, refresh in cold water and carefully pat dry.

2 Grease a 1kg/2lb loaf tin and line the base with a sheet of greaseproof paper. Line with the spinach leaves, allowing them to overhang the tin.

3 Blanch the rest of the vegetables in boiling, salted water until just tender. Drain and refresh in cold water then, when cool, pat dry with pieces of kitchen paper.

4 Place the vegetables into the loaf tin in a colourful mixture, making sure the sticks of vegetables lie lengthways.

5 Beat the sauce ingredients together and slowly pour over the vegetables. Tap the loaf tin to ensure the sauce seeps into the gaps. Fold over the spinach leaves at the top of the terrine to make a neat surface.

6 Cover the terrine with a sheet of greased foil, then bake in a roasting tin half full of boiling water for about 1–1¼ hours until set.

7 Cool the terrine in the tin, then chill. To serve, loosen the sides and shake out gently. Serve cut in thick slices.

HAM AND BULGUR WHEAT SALAD

This flavoursome, nutty salad is ideal for using up leftover cooked ham for a quick and

simple addition to a Christmas buffet menu.

INGREDIENTS

225g/8oz/1⅓ cup bulgur wheat
45ml/3 tbsp olive oil
30ml/2 tbsp lemon juice
1 red (bell) pepper
225g/8oz cooked ham, diced
30ml/2 tbsp chopped fresh mint
30ml/2 tbsp currants
salt and freshly ground black pepper
sprigs of fresh mint and lemon slices,
to garnish

Serves 8

3 Quarter the pepper, removing the stalk and seeds. Rinse under running water. Using a sharp knife, cut the pepper quarters into wide strips and then into diamonds.

4 Add the pepper, ham, chopped fresh mint and currants to the wheat in the bowl. Mix with a spoon to ensure the ingredients are well distributed, then transfer the salad to a serving dish, garnish with the fresh mint sprigs and lemon slices and serve.

VARIATION

This salad can also be made with 225g/8oz/1⅓ cup couscous instead of the bulgur wheat. To prepare, cover the couscous with boiling water as in Step 1.

1 Put the bulgur wheat into a bowl, pour over enough boiling water to cover and leave to stand until all the water has been absorbed and the grains look as if they have swelled up.

2 Add the oil, lemon juice, and seasoning to taste. Toss to separate the grains using two forks.

Puddings and Desserts

Christmas is a time to indulge in sweet things. At Christmas Dinner, most guests will expect Traditional Christmas Pudding, but other variations on the festive theme such as Chocolate and Chestnut Yule Log or Christmas Cranberry Bombe can be just as welcome. After a heavy meal, a fruit-based dessert like Ruby Fruit Salad or Spiced Pears in Red Wine will always be appreciated, and, for successful entertaining, try individual desserts such as sinful Frozen Grand Marnier Soufflés, laced with alcohol. Specialities for chocaholics include Chocolate Sorbet, while Chocolate Crêpes with Plums and Port will provide a sophisticated end to any festive meal.

TRADITIONAL CHRISTMAS PUDDING

This recipe makes enough to fill one 1.2 litre/2 pint/5 cup basin or two 600ml/1 pint/2½ cup basins.

It can be made up to a month before Christmas, steamed for 6 to 8 hours, then stored in a

cool, dry place. Serve topped with a decorative sprig of holly.

INGREDIENTS

115g/4oz/½ cup butter
*225g/8oz/1 heaped cup soft dark
brown sugar*
*50g/2oz/½ cup self-raising
(self-rising) flour*
5ml/1 tsp mixed spice
1.5ml/¼ tsp nutmeg
2.5ml/½ tsp ground cinnamon
2 eggs
115g/4oz/2 cups fresh white breadcrumbs
175g/6oz/1 cup sultanas (golden raisins)
175g/6oz/1 cup raisins
115g/4oz/½ cup currants
*25g/1oz/3 tbsp mixed chopped
(candied) peel*
25g/1oz/¼ cup chopped almonds
*1 small cooking apple, peeled, cored and
coarsely grated*
finely grated rind of 1 orange or lemon
*juice of 1 orange or lemon, made up to
150ml/¼ pint/⅔ cup with brandy or rum*

Serves 8

1 Cut a disc of greaseproof paper to fit the base of the basin(s) and butter the disc and basin(s).

2 Whisk the butter and sugar together until soft. Beat in the flour, spices and eggs. Stir in the remaining ingredients thoroughly. The mixture should have a soft dropping consistency.

3 Turn the mixture into the greased basin(s) and level the top.

4 Cover with another disc of buttered greaseproof paper.

5 Make a pleat across the centre of a large piece of greaseproof paper and cover the basin(s), tying it with string. Pleat a piece of foil in the same way and cover the basin(s), tucking it under the greaseproof frill.

6 Tie another piece of string around the basin(s) and across the top, as a handle. Place the basin(s) in a steamer over a pan of simmering water and steam for 6 hours. If you do not have a steamer, put the basin(s) into a large pan and pour round enough boiling water to come halfway up the basin(s) and cover the pan with a tight-fitting lid.

7 Check the water is simmering and top it up with boiling water as it evaporates. When the pudding(s) have cooked, after about 2 hours, leave to cool completely. Then remove the foil and greaseproof paper. Wipe the basin(s) clean and replace the greaseproof paper and foil, ready for reheating when required.

COOK'S TIP

To serve, steam for 2 hours. Turn on to a plate and leave to stand for 5 minutes before removing the pudding basin (the steam will rise to the top of the basin and help to loosen the pudding).

CRÊPES WITH ORANGE SAUCE

This is a sophisticated dessert that is easy to make at home. You can make

the crêpes in advance; you will be able to put the dish together quickly at the last minute.

INGREDIENTS

115g/4oz/⅔ cup plain (all-purpose) flour
1.5ml/¼ tsp salt
25g/1oz/2 tbsp caster (superfine) sugar
2 eggs, lightly beaten
250ml/8fl oz/1 cup milk
60ml/4 tbsp water
30ml/2 tbsp orange flower water or orange
liqueur (optional)
25g/1oz/2 tbsp unsalted butter, melted,
plus more for frying

For the Orange Sauce
75g/3oz/6 tbsp unsalted butter
55g/2oz/¼ cup caster (superfine) sugar
grated rind and juice of 1 large
unwaxed orange
grated rind and juice of
1 unwaxed lemon
150ml/¼ pint/⅔ cup fresh orange juice
60ml/4 tbsp orange liqueur
brandy and orange liqueur,
for flaming (optional)
orange segments, to decorate

Serves 6

2 Heat an 18–20cm/7–8in crêpe pan (preferably non-stick) over a medium heat. Stir the melted butter into the crêpe batter. Brush the hot pan with a little extra melted butter and pour in about 30ml/2 tbsp of batter. Quickly tilt and rotate the pan to cover the base with a thin layer of batter. Cook for about 1 minute until the top is set and the base is golden. With a palette knife, lift the edge to check the colour, then carefully turn over the crêpe and cook for 20–30 seconds, just to set. Transfer the crêpe to a plate.

4 To make the sauce, melt the butter in a large frying pan over a medium-low heat, then stir in the sugar, orange and lemon rind and juice, the additional orange juice and the orange liqueur, if using.

5 Place a crêpe in the pan browned-side down, swirling gently to coat with the sauce. Fold it in half, then in half again to form a triangle and push to the side of the pan. Continue heating and folding the crêpes until all are warm and covered with the sauce.

1 Sift together the flour, salt and sugar. Make a well in the centre and pour in the eggs. Beat the eggs, whisking in the flour until it is all incorporated. Whisk in the milk and water until smooth. Whisk in the orange flower water or liqueur. Then strain the batter into a jug and set aside.

3 Continue cooking the crêpes, stirring the batter occasionally and brushing the pan with a little melted butter as and when necessary. Place a sheet of clear film between each crêpe as they are stacked to prevent sticking. (Crêpes can be prepared ahead to this point – wrap and chill until ready to use.)

6 If you want to flame the crêpes, heat 30–45ml/2–3tbsp each of orange liqueur and brandy in a small saucepan over a medium heat. Remove the pan from the heat, carefully ignite the liquid with a match then gently pour over the crêpes. Scatter over the orange segments and serve at once.

CHOCOLATE CRÊPES WITH PLUMS AND PORT

A sumptuous dinner party dessert, this dish can be made in advance and will always

impress your guests. It is, however, easy to make and looks very attractive.

INGREDIENTS

*50g/2oz plain (semisweet) chocolate,
broken up*
200ml/7fl oz/scant 1 cup milk
120ml/4fl oz/½ cup single (light) cream
30ml/2 tbsp cocoa powder
115g/4oz/1 cup plain (all-purpose) flour
2 eggs
oil, for frying

For the Filling
500g/1¼ lb red or golden plums
50g/2oz/¼ cup caster (superfine) sugar
30ml/2 tbsp each water and port
175g/6oz/¾ cup crème fraîche

For the Sauce
*150g/5oz plain (semisweet) chocolate,
broken up*
175ml/6fl oz/¾ cup double (heavy) cream
30ml/2 tbsp port

Serves 6

1 Place the chocolate in a saucepan with the milk. Heat gently until the chocolate has melted completely. Pour into a blender or food processor and add the cream, cocoa powder, flour and eggs. Process the mixture until smooth, then tip into a jug and chill for 30 minutes.

2 Meanwhile, make the filling. Halve and stone the plums. Place them in a saucepan and add the sugar and water. Bring to the boil, then cover and simmer for 10 minutes. Stir in the port; simmer for a further 30 seconds. Remove from the heat and keep warm.

3 Have ready a sheet of non-stick baking paper. Heat a crêpe pan, grease it with a little oil, then pour in just enough batter to cover the base of the pan, swirling to coat evenly. Cook until the crêpe has set, then flip it over to cook the other side. Slide it out on to the paper, then cook 9–11 more.

4 Make the chocolate sauce. Combine the chocolate and cream in a saucepan. Heat gently, stirring until smooth. Add the port and heat gently for 1 minute.

5 Divide the filling among the crêpes, add crème fraîche to each and roll them up. Serve with the chocolate sauce.

Chocolate, Date and Almond Filo Coil

Experience the allure of the Middle East with this delectable dessert. Crisp filo pastry conceals

a chocolate and rose water filling studded with dates and almonds.

Ingredients

275g/10oz packet filo pastry, thawed if frozen
50g/2oz/4 tbsp unsalted butter, melted
icing sugar, cocoa powder and ground cinnamon, for dusting

For the Filling
75g/3oz/6 tbsp unsalted butter
115g/4oz plain (semisweet) chocolate, broken into squares
115g/4oz/1 cup ground almonds
115g/4oz/⅔ cup chopped dates
75g/3oz/⅔ cup icing (confectioner's) sugar
10ml/2 tsp rose water
2.5ml/½ tsp ground cinnamon

Serves 6

1 Preheat the oven to 180°C/350°F/ Gas 4. Grease a 22cm/8½in round cake tin. Make the chocolate, date and almond filling. Melt the butter with the chocolate in a heatproof bowl over a saucepan of barely simmering water, then remove the saucepan from the heat and stir in all of the remaining ingredients to make a thick paste. Set the pan aside to cool.

2 Lay one sheet of the filo pastry on a clean work surface. Brush the filo with the melted butter, then lay a second sheet of filo on top and brush again with butter.

3 Roll a handful of the chocolate almond mixture into a long sausage shape and place along one edge of the filo. Roll the pastry tightly around.

4 Place the roll around the outside of the tin. Make enough rolls to fill the tin.

5 Brush the coil with the remaining melted butter. Bake for 30–35 minutes until the pastry is golden brown and crisp. Remove the coil from the tin; place it on a plate. Serve warm, dusted with icing sugar, cocoa and cinnamon.

CRUNCHY APPLE AND ALMOND FLAN

Do not be tempted to put any sugar with the apples, as this makes them produce too much liquid. All the sweetness you'll need is in the pastry and topping.

INGREDIENTS

75g/3oz/6 tbsp butter
175g/6oz/1½ cups plain (all-purpose) flour
25g/1oz/scant ⅓ cup ground almonds
25g/1oz/2 tbsp caster (superfine) sugar
1 egg yolk
15ml/1 tbsp cold water
1.5ml/¼ tsp almond essence
sifted icing sugar, to decorate

For the Crunchy Topping
115g/4oz/1 cup plain (all-purpose) flour
1.5ml/¼ tsp mixed spice
50g/2oz/4 tbsp butter, cut in small cubes
50g/2oz/4 tbsp demerara (raw) sugar
50g/2oz/½ cup flaked almonds

For the filling
675g/1½lb cooking apples
25g/1oz/2 tbsp raisins

Serves 8

1 To make the pastry, rub the butter into the flour, either with your fingertips in a large mixing bowl or in a food processor, until it resembles fine breadcrumbs. Stir in the ground almonds and sugar. Whisk the egg yolk, water and almond essence together and mix them into the dry ingredients to form a soft, pliable dough. Knead the dough lightly until smooth, wrap in clear film and leave in a cool place or in the refrigerator to rest for about 20 minutes.

2 Meanwhile, make the crunchy topping. Sift the flour and mixed spice into a bowl and rub in the butter. Stir in the sugar and almonds.

3 Roll out the pastry on a lightly floured surface and use it to line a 23cm/9in loose-based flan tin, taking care to press it neatly into the edges and to make a lip around the top edge.

4 Roll off the excess pastry to neaten the edge. Allow to chill in the refrigerator for about 15 minutes.

COOK'S TIP

Pears would also be delicious in this flan, or you could use a mixture of apples and pears.

5 Preheat the oven to 190°C/375°F/ Gas 5. Preheat a baking sheet in the oven. Peel, core and slice the apples thinly. In the flan, arrange them in overlapping, concentric circles, so that there is a slightly raised area in the centre. Scatter over the raisins. The flan will seem too full at this stage, but as the apples cook and shrink, the filling will drop slightly.

6 Cover the apples with the crunchy topping mixture, pressing it on lightly. Bake on the hot baking sheet for 25–30 minutes, or until the top is golden brown and the apples are tender (test them with a fine skewer). Leave the flan to cool completely in the tin for 10 minutes before turning out. The flan can be served either warm or cool, dusted with a little sifted icing sugar.

Mango and Amaretti Strudel

Fresh mango and crushed amaretti wrapped in wafer-thin filo pastry make a

seasonal treat that is equally delicious made with apricots or plums.

INGREDIENTS

1 large mango
grated rind of 1 lemon
2 amaretti
25g/1oz/3 tbsp demerara (raw) sugar
60ml/4 tbsp wholemeal
(whole-wheat) breadcrumbs
2 sheets of filo pastry
20g/¾oz/4 tsp soft margarine, melted
15ml/1 tbsp chopped almonds
icing (confectioner's) sugar, for dusting

Serves 4

1 Preheat the oven to 190ºC/375ºF/
Gas 5. Lightly grease a large baking
sheet. Halve, stone and peel the
mango. Cut the flesh into cubes,
then place them in a bowl and
sprinkle with the grated lemon rind.

2 Crush the amaretti with a rolling
pin, transfer to a bowl and mix them
with the demerara sugar and the
wholemeal breadcrumbs.

3 Lay one sheet of filo on a flat surface
and brush with a quarter of the melted
margarine. Top with the second sheet,
brush with one-third of the remaining
margarine, then fold both sheets over,
if necessary, to make a rectangle
measuring 28 x 24cm/11 x 9½in.
Brush the rectangle with half the
remaining margarine.

4 Sprinkle the filo with the amaretti
mixture, leaving a 5cm/2in border on
each long side. Arrange the mango
cubes over the top.

5 Roll up the filo from one of the
long sides, Swiss roll fashion. Lift
the strudel on to the baking sheet
with the join underneath. Brush with
the remaining melted margarine and
sprinkle with the chopped almonds.

6 Bake the strudel for 20–25 minutes
until golden brown, then carefully
transfer it to a board. Dust the strudel
with the icing sugar, slice diagonally
and serve warm.

COOK'S TIP

*The easiest way to prepare a
mango is to cut horizontally through
the fruit, keeping the knife blade
close to the stone. Repeat on the
other side of the stone and peel off
the skin. Remove the remaining skin
and flesh from around the stone.*

CHRISTMAS CRANBERRY BOMBE

This is a light alternative to Christmas pudding that is made with very seasonal ingredients.

It also looks attractively festive and tastes delicious.

INGREDIENTS

For the Sorbet Centre
225g/8oz/2 cups cranberries
150ml/¼ pint/⅔ cup orange juice
finely grated rind of ½ orange
2.5ml/½ tsp allspice
60ml/4 tbsp demerara (raw) sugar

For the Outer Layer
600ml/1 pint/2⅔ cups vanilla ice cream
30ml/2 tbsp chopped angelica
30ml/2 tbsp (candied) citrus peel
15ml/1 tbsp flaked (sliced) almonds, toasted

Serves 6

1 Put the cranberries, orange juice, peel and spice in a pan and cook gently until the cranberries are soft. Add the sugar, then purée in a food processor until almost smooth, but still with some texture. Leave to cool.

2 Allow the vanilla ice cream to soften slightly then stir in the chopped angelica, mixed peel and almonds.

3 Pack the mixture into a 5 cup pudding mould and, using a metal spoon, hollow out the centre. Freeze the mould until firm to the touch. This will take at least 3 hours.

4 Fill the hollowed-out centre of the bombe with cranberry mixture, smooth over and freeze until firm. To serve, allow to soften slightly at room temperature, turn out and slice.

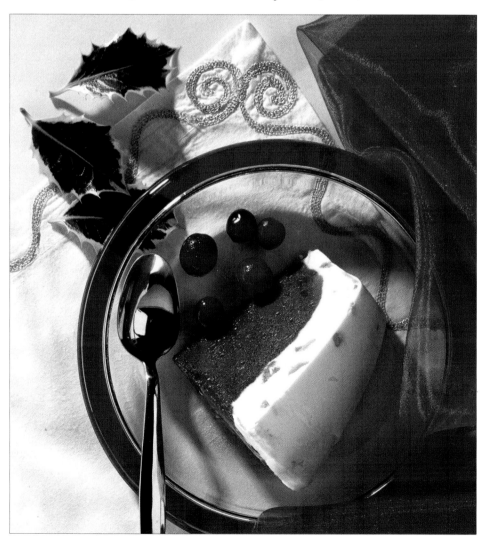

Chocolate Sorbet

This is a classical favourite for chocolate lovers and makes a light ending to a meal.

It has the added advantage that you can make it well ahead and bring it out when needed.

INGREDIENTS

*150g/5oz dark (bittersweet)
chocolate, chopped
115g/4oz plain (semisweet)
chocolate, grated
225g/8oz/1 cup caster
(superfine) sugar
475ml/16fl oz/2 cups water
chocolate curls, to decorate*

Serves 6

1 Put all of the chocolate in a food processor, fitted with a metal blade, and process for approximately 20–30 seconds, or until it is very finely chopped.

2 Place the sugar and water in a pan over medium heat. Bring to the boil, stirring until all of the sugar has completely dissolved. Boil for about 2 minutes, then remove the pan from the heat.

3 While the machine is running, carefully add the hot sugar-and-water syrup to the chocolate in the food processor. Keep the food processor running for 1–2 minutes until the chocolate is completely melted and the mixture is smooth. Using a rubber spatula, scrape down the bowl once or twice to catch any mixture that is clinging to the sides.

4 Strain the chocolate mixture into a large measuring jug (cup). Cool, then chill, and stir the mixture occasionally. Pour the mixture into a freezer container and freeze until slushy. Whisk until smooth, then freeze again until almost firm. Whisk it for a second time and return it to the freezer. Allow to soften slightly before serving decorated with the chocolate curls.

CHOCOLATE ROULADE WITH COCONUT CREAM

This sinfully rich roulade is the ultimate in Christmas treats. Eaten in small slices, it makes the

perfect dessert for any festive or celebratory dinner party.

INGREDIENTS

50g/5oz/¾ cup caster (superfine) sugar
5 eggs, separated
50g/2oz/½ cup cocoa powder

For the Filling
300ml/½ pint/1¼ cups double
(heavy) cream
45ml/3 tbsp whisky
50g/2oz piece solid creamed coconut
30ml/2 tbsp caster sugar

For the Topping
coarsely grated curls of fresh coconut
chocolate curls

Serves 8

1 Preheat the oven to 180°C/350°F/ Gas 4. Grease a 33 x 23cm/13 x 9in Swiss roll tin. Dust a sheet of greaseproof paper with 30ml/2 tbsp of sugar.

2 Place the egg yolks in a heatproof bowl. Add the remaining caster sugar and whisk with a hand-held electric mixer until the mixture is thick enough to leave a trail. Sift the cocoa over, then fold in carefully and evenly with a metal spoon.

3 Whisk the egg whites in a clean, grease-free bowl until they form soft peaks. Fold about 15ml/1 tbsp of the whites into the chocolate mixture to lighten it, then fold in the rest evenly.

4 Scrape the mixture into the prepared tin, taking it right into the corners. Smooth the surface with a palette knife, then bake for 20–25 minutes or until well risen and springy to the touch.

5 Turn the cooked sponge out on to the sugar-dusted greaseproof paper and carefully peel off the lining paper. Cover with a damp, clean dish towel and leave to cool.

COOK'S TIP

Either Irish or Scotch Whisky can be used to make the cream filling for this dessert. If whisky is not available, you can use white rum or a rum-based spirit, such as Malibu, as a suitable alternative.

6 To make the filling, whisk the cream with the whisky in a bowl until the mixture just holds its shape, then finely grate the creamed coconut and stir it in with the sugar.

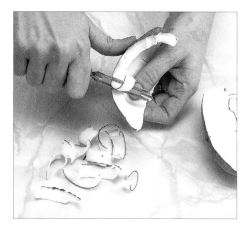

7 Remove the dish towel to uncover the sponge. Spread about three-quarters of the cream mixture to the edges of the sponge. Roll up carefully from a long side. Transfer the roulade to a plate and pipe or spoon the remaining cream mixture on top. Then grate the fresh coconut to make the curls and place them on top, along with the chocolate curls.

RASPBERRY AND WHITE CHOCOLATE CHEESECAKE

Raspberries and white chocolate are an irresistible combination, especially when

teamed with smooth, rich mascarpone cheese on a crunchy ginger and pecan nut base.

INGREDIENTS

50g/2oz/4 tbsp unsalted butter
225g/8oz ginger nut biscuits
(gingersnaps), crushed
50g/2oz/½ cup chopped pecan nuts
or walnuts

For the Filling
275g/10oz/1¼ cups mascarpone
175g/6oz/¾ cup fromage frais
(farmer's cheese)
2 eggs, beaten
45ml/3 tbsp caster (superfine) sugar
250g/9oz white chocolate, chopped
225g/8oz/1½ cups fresh or
frozen raspberries

For the Topping
115g/4 oz/½ cups mascarpone
75g/3oz/⅓ cup fromage frais
(farmer's cheese)
white chocolate curls and raspberries,
to decorate

Serves 8

1 Preheat the oven to 150°C/300°F/ Gas 2. Melt the butter in a large saucepan, then stir in the crushed biscuits and nuts. Press the mixture into the base of a 23cm/9in springform cake tin.

2 To make the filling, beat the mascarpone cheese and fromage frais in a large bowl, then gradually beat in the eggs and caster sugar until all the ingredients are evenly mixed.

3 Melt the white chocolate very gently in a heatproof bowl over hot water, then stir into the cheese mixture with the fresh or frozen raspberries.

4 Transfer the mixture to the prepared tin and spread evenly with a palette knife, then bake for about 1 hour or until just set. Switch off the oven, but do not remove the cheesecake. Leave it in the oven until it is cold and completely set.

5 Remove the sides of the tin and carefully lift the cheesecake on to a serving plate. Make the topping by mixing together the mascarpone and fromage frais in a bowl and spreading the mixture over the cheesecake. Decorate with white chocolate curls and the fresh raspberries.

COOK'S TIPS

The biscuits for the base should be crushed quite finely. This can easily be done in a food processor. Alternatively, just place the biscuits in a stout plastic bag, tied so that no crumbs can escape, and crush them with a rolling pin.

Take care when melting white chocolate; it is very sensitive to heat and easily scorches and can separate if overheated. Don't allow any water, even the smallest splash, to come into contact with the chocolate because it will cause the chocolate to become lumpy and grainy and unworkable. To avoid this, start off with a dry bowl, don't cover it, and keep the water at a very gentle simmer.

Amaretto Mousses with Chocolate Sauce

These little desserts are extremely rich and derive their flavour from Amaretto, an

almond-flavoured liqueur, and amaretti, little almond-flavoured biscuits.

INGREDIENTS

*115g/4oz amaretti, ratafias
or macaroons
60ml/4 tbsp Amaretto di Sarone
350g/12oz white chocolate, broken
into squares
15g/½oz powdered gelatine, soaked in
45ml/3 tbsp cold water
450ml/¾ pint/1⅞ cups double
(heavy) cream*

For the Chocolate Sauce
*225g/8oz dark (bittersweet) chocolate,
broken into squares
300ml/½ pint/1¼ cups single (light) cream
50g/2oz/4 tbsp caster (superfine) sugar*

Serves 8

1 Lightly oil eight individual 120ml/ 4fl oz/½ cup moulds and line the base of each mould with a small disc of oiled greaseproof paper. Put the biscuits into a large bowl and crush them finely with a rolling pin.

2 Melt the Amaretto and white chocolate together gently in a bowl over a pan of hot but not boiling water (be very careful not to overheat the chocolate or it will begin to separate and go unpleasantly grainy). Stir well until smooth; remove from the pan and leave to cool.

3 Melt the gelatine over hot water and blend it into the chocolate mixture. Whisk the cream until it holds soft peaks. Gently fold in the chocolate mixture, with 60ml/4 tbsp of the crushed biscuits.

4 Put a teaspoonful of the crushed biscuits into the bottom of each mould and spoon in the chocolate mixture. Tap each mould to disperse any air bubbles. Level the tops and sprinkle the remaining crushed biscuits on top. Press down gently and chill for 4 hours.

5 To make the chocolate sauce, put all the ingredients in a saucepan and heat gently to melt the chocolate and dissolve the sugar. Simmer for 2–3 minutes. Leave to cool completely.

6 Slip a knife around the sides of each mould, and turn out on to individual plates. Remove the greaseproof paper from the bottom and pour round a little dark chocolate sauce.

> ### COOK'S TIP
> *When melting chocolate, always set the bowl over a half-full pan of barely simmering water; chocolate reacts badly to splashes of water and overheating.*

Iced Praline Torte

Make this elaborate torte several days ahead, decorate it and return it to the freezer until you

are nearly ready to serve it. Allow the torte to stand at room temperature for an hour before

serving, or leave it in the refrigerator overnight to soften.

Ingredients

115g/4oz/1 cup almonds or hazelnuts
115g/4oz/8 tbsp caster (superfine) sugar
115g/4oz/⅔ cup raisins
90ml/6 tbsp rum or brandy
115g/4oz plain (semisweet) chocolate,
broken into squares
30ml/2 tbsp milk
450ml/¾ pint/1⅞ cups double
(heavy) cream
30ml/2 tbsp strong black coffee
16 sponge-finger biscuits

To Finish
150ml/¼ pint/⅔ cup double
(heavy) cream
50g/2oz/½ cup flaked almonds, toasted
15g/½oz plain (semisweet)
chocolate, melted

Serves 8

1 To make the praline, have ready an oiled baking sheet. Put the nuts into a heavy-based saucepan with the sugar and heat until the sugar melts. Swirl to coat the nuts in the hot sugar. Cook slowly until the nuts brown and the sugar caramelizes. This will only take a few minutes. Turn the nuts on to the baking sheet and leave to cool. When cool, break the praline up and grind it to a fine powder in a food processor.

2 Soak the raisins in 45ml/3 tbsp of the rum or brandy for an hour (or better still overnight), so they soften and absorb the full flavour of the alcohol. Melt the chocolate with the milk in a bowl over a pan of barely simmering water. Remove and allow to cool. Lightly grease a 1.2 litre/2 pint/5 cup loaf tin and line it with greaseproof paper.

3 Whisk the cream in a bowl until it holds soft peaks. Whisk in the cold chocolate. Then fold in the praline and the soaked raisins, with any liquid.

4 Mix the coffee and remaining rum or brandy in a shallow dish. Dip in each of the sponge-finger biscuits and arrange half in a layer over the base of the prepared loaf tin.

5 Cover the sponge biscuits with the chocolate mixture and add another layer of soaked sponge fingers. Freeze overnight.

6 Dip the cake tin briefly into warm water to loosen it and turn the torte out on to a serving plate. Cover with whipped cream. Sprinkle the top with toasted flaked almonds and drizzle the melted chocolate over the top. Return the torte to the freezer until it is needed.

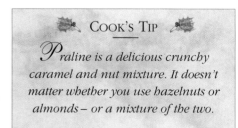

COOK'S TIP

Praline is a delicious crunchy caramel and nut mixture. It doesn't matter whether you use hazelnuts or almonds – or a mixture of the two.

Frozen Grand Marnier Soufflés

These luxurious individual little puddings are always appreciated and make a wonderful

finale for any Christmas-time meal.

INGREDIENTS

200g/7oz/1 cup caster (superfine) sugar
6 large eggs, separated
250ml/8fl oz/1 cup milk
15g/½oz powdered gelatine, soaked in
45ml/3 tbsp cold water
450ml/¾ pint/1⅞ cups double
(heavy) cream
60ml/4 tbsp Grand Marnier

Serves 8

1 Fold a double collar of greaseproof paper around eight ramekin dishes and tie with string. Put 75g/3oz/6 tbsp of the caster sugar in a bowl with the egg yolks and whisk until the yolks are pale. This will take about 3 minutes if you use an electric hand mixer.

2 Heat the milk until almost boiling and pour it on to the yolks, whisking. Return to the pan and stir over a gentle heat until thick enough to coat the back of the spoon. Remove from the heat, and add the soaked gelatine. Pour into a bowl and cool. Whisk occasionally, until the custard is about to set.

3 Put the remaining sugar in a pan with the water and dissolve over low heat. Bring to the boil and boil rapidly until it reaches the soft ball stage or 119°C/238°F on a sugar thermometer. Remove from the heat. In a clean bowl, whisk the egg whites until they are stiff. Pour the syrup on to the whites, while whisking. Cool.

4 Whisk the cream until it holds soft peaks. Add the Grand Marnier to the cold custard and fold into the cold meringue, with the cream. Pour into the ramekin dishes. Freeze overnight. Remove the collars. Leave at room temperature for 30 minutes, then serve.

COOK'S TIP

The soft ball stage of a syrup is when a teaspoon of the mixture dropped into a glass of cold water solidifies into a ball.

Mini Millefeuille

This pâtisserie *classic is a delectable combination of tender puff pastry sandwiched with luscious*

pastry cream. It is difficult to cut, making individual servings a brilliant solution.

INGREDIENTS

*450g/1lb rough-puff or
puff pastry
6 egg yolks
70g/2½oz/⅓ cup caster (superfine) sugar
45ml/3 tbsp plain (all-purpose) flour
350ml/12fl oz/1½ cups milk
30ml/2 tbsp Kirsch or cherry
liqueur (optional)
450g/1lb/2⅔ cups raspberries
icing (confectioner's) sugar, for dusting
strawberry or raspberry coulis,
to serve*

Serves 8

1 Lightly butter two large baking sheets and then sprinkle them very lightly with cold water.

2 On a lightly floured surface, roll out the pastry to a 3mm/⅛in thickness. Using a 10cm/4in cutter, cut out 12 rounds. Place the rounds on the baking sheets and prick each with a fork. Chill the rounds for 30 minutes. Preheat the oven to 200°C/400°F/Gas 6.

3 Bake the pastry rounds for about 15–20 minutes until golden, then transfer to wire racks to cool.

4 Whisk the egg yolks and sugar until light and creamy, then whisk in the flour until blended. Bring the milk to the boil and pour it over the egg mixture, whisking. Return to the saucepan, bring to the boil and boil for 2 minutes, whisking. Remove the pan from the heat and whisk in the Kirsch or liqueur. Pour into a bowl and press clear film on to the surface to prevent a skin forming. Set aside to cool.

5 To assemble, split the pastry rounds in half, into 24 rounds. Spread one round at a time with a little pastry cream. Arrange a layer of raspberries over the cream and top with a second pastry round. Spread with more cream and a few more raspberries. Top with a third pastry round flat side up. Dust with icing sugar and serve with coulis.

CHOCOLATE AND CHESTNUT YULE LOG

This chocolate log is traditionally served at Christmas. Make it the day before it is needed

or some time in advance and freeze it. It makes an excellent dessert for a party.

INGREDIENTS

25g/1oz/2 tbsp plain (all-purpose) flour
30ml/2 tbsp cocoa powder
pinch of salt
3 large eggs, separated
large pinch of cream of tartar
115g/4oz/8 tbsp caster (superfine) sugar
2–3 drops almond essence
sifted cocoa powder and holly sprigs,
to decorate

For the Filling

15ml/1 tbsp rum or brandy
5ml/1 tsp powdered gelatine
115g/4oz plain (semisweet) chocolate,
broken into squares
50g/2oz/4 tbsp caster (superfine) sugar
250g/8oz can chestnut purée
225ml/½ pint/1¼ cups double
(heavy) cream

Serves 8

1 Preheat the oven to 180°C/350°F/ Gas 4. Grease and line a 23 x 33cm/ 9 x 13in Swiss roll tin and line the base with non-stick baking paper. Sift the flour, cocoa and salt together on to a piece of greaseproof paper.

2 Put the egg whites into a large clean bowl and whisk them until frothy. Add the cream of tartar and whisk until stiff. Gradually whisk in half the sugar, until the mixture will stand in stiff peaks.

3 Put the egg yolks and the remaining sugar into another bowl and whisk until thick and pale. Add the almond essence. Stir in the sifted flour and cocoa mixture. Lastly, fold in the egg whites, using a metal spoon, until everything is evenly blended. Be careful not to over-mix.

4 Transfer the mixture to the prepared Swiss roll tin and level the top. Bake for 15–20 minutes, or until springy to the touch. Have ready a large piece of greaseproof paper dusted liberally with caster sugar. Turn the Swiss roll on to the paper, remove the baking lining paper, and roll it up with the greaseproof paper still inside. Leave to cool completely on a wire rack.

5 Put the rum or brandy in a cup and sprinkle over the gelatine; leave to become spongy. Melt the chocolate in a 600ml/1 pint/2½ cup basin over a pan of hot water. Melt the gelatine over barely simmering water and add to the chocolate.

6 Using an electric beater, whisk the sugar and chestnut purée into the chocolate mixture. Remove the basin from the heat and leave to cool. Whisk the cream until it holds soft peaks. Fold the two mixtures together evenly.

7 Unroll the Swiss roll carefully, spread it with half the filling and roll it up again. Place it on a serving dish and spread over the rest of the chocolate cream to cover it. Mark it with a fork to resemble a log. Chill until firm. Dust the cake with sifted cocoa powder and decorate around the edges of the plate with sprigs of holly.

GINGER TRIFLE

This is a good way to use up leftover cake, whether plain, chocolate or gingerbread. You can substitute

runny honey for the ginger and syrup, if you prefer. This pudding can be made the day before.

INGREDIENTS

225g/8oz gingerbread or other cake
60ml/4 tbsp Grand Marnier or sherry
2 ripe dessert pears, peeled, cored
and cubed
2 bananas, thickly sliced
2 oranges, segmented
1–2 pieces preserved stem ginger, chopped,
plus 30ml/2 tbsp syrup

For the Custard
2 eggs
50g/2oz/4 tbsp caster (superfine) sugar
15ml/1 tbsp cornflour (cornstarch)
450ml/¾ pint/1⅞ cups milk
few drops vanilla extract

To Decorate
150ml/¼ pint/⅔ cup double (heavy)
cream, lightly whipped
25g/1oz/¼ cup chopped almonds, toasted
4 glacé (candied) cherries
8 small pieces (candied) angelica

Serves 8

3 Mix all the prepared fruit with the ginger and syrup. Spoon into the bowl on top of the gingerbread. Spoon over the custard to cover and chill until set.

4 Cover the top with whipped cream and scatter on the toasted almonds. Arrange the glacé cherries and angelica around the edge.

1 Cut the gingerbread into 4cm/1½in cubes. Put them in the bottom of a 1.75 litre/3 pint/7½ cup glass bowl. Sprinkle over the liqueur and set aside.

2 For the custard, whisk the eggs, sugar and cornflour into a pan with a little milk. Heat the remaining milk until almost boiling. Pour it on to the egg mixture, whisking. Heat, stirring, until thickened. Simmer for 2 minutes. Add the vanilla essence and leave to cool.

Ruby Fruit Salad

After a rich main course, this port-flavoured fruit salad is light and refreshing.

You can use any fruit that is available.

INGREDIENTS

300ml/½ pint/1¼ cups water
115g/4oz/8 tbsp caster (superfine) sugar
1 cinnamon stick
4 cloves
pared rind of 1 orange
300ml/½ pint/1¼ cups port
2 oranges
1 small ripe Ogen, Charentais or
Honeydew melon
4 small bananas
2 dessert apples
225g/8oz seedless grapes

Serves 8

1 Put the water, sugar, spices and pared orange rind into a saucepan and stir, over a gentle heat, to dissolve the sugar. Then bring the liquid to the boil, cover the pan with a lid and allow to simmer gently for 10 minutes. Remove the pan from the heat and set aside to cool, then add the port.

2 Strain the liquid through a sieve into a mixing bowl, to remove the spices and orange rind. With a sharp knife, cut off all the skin and pith from the oranges. Then, holding each orange over the bowl to catch the juice, cut away the segments, by slicing between the membrane that divides each segment and allowing the segments to drop into the syrup. Squeeze the remaining pith to release as much of the remaining juice as possible.

3 On a chopping board, cut the melon in half, remove the seeds and scoop out the flesh with a melon baller, or cut it into small cubes. Add it to the syrup. Peel the bananas and cut them in 1cm/½in slices.

4 Quarter and core the apples and cut them in small cubes. (Leave the skin on, or peel if the skin is tough.) Halve the grapes if large, or leave them whole. Stir all the fruit into the syrup, cover and chill for an hour before serving.

GOLDEN GINGER COMPOTE

This compote is as good to eat as it looks. Warm, spicy and full of sun-ripened

ingredients, it is the perfect Christmas dessert.

INGREDIENTS

2 cups kumquats
150g/5oz/1¼ cups dried apricots
25g/1oz/2 tbsp raisins
400ml/14fl oz/1⅔ cups water
1 orange
2.5cm/1in piece fresh root ginger, peeled
and grated
4 cardamom pods, crushed
4 cloves
30ml/2 tbsp honey
15g/½oz/1 tbsp flaked (sliced)
almonds, toasted

1 Wash the kumquats, and, if they are large, cut them in half. Place them in a pan with the apricots, raisins and water. Bring to the boil.

2 Pare the rind from the orange and add to the pan. Add the ginger, the cardamom pods and the cloves.

3 Reduce the heat, cover and simmer for about 30 minutes or until tender.

4 Add the orange juice to the pan with honey. Add the almonds and serve.

COOK'S TIP

Reduce the liquid to 300ml/½ pint/1¼ cups, and add ready-to-eat apricots for the last 5 minutes.

Spiced Pears in Red Wine

Serve these pears hot or cold, with lightly whipped cream. The flavours improve with

keeping, so you can make this several days before you want to serve it.

INGREDIENTS

600ml/1 pint/2½ cups red wine
225g/8oz/1 cup caster (superfine) sugar
cinnamon stick
6 cloves
finely grated rind of 1 orange
10ml/2 tsp grated fresh root ginger
8 even-sized firm pears, with stalks
15ml/1 tbsp brandy
25g/1oz/2 tbsp almonds or hazelnuts,
toasted, to decorate

Serves 8

1 Choose a pan large enough to hold all the pears upright in one layer. Put all the ingredients except the pears, brandy and almonds into the pan and heat slowly until the sugar has dissolved. Simmer for 5 minutes.

2 Peel the pears, leaving the stalks on, and cut away the flower end. Arrange them upright in the pan. Cover with a lid and simmer until they are tender. The cooking time will depend on their size, but will be about 45–50 minutes.

3 Remove the pears from the syrup, using a slotted spoon, being careful not to pull out the stalks. Put the pears in one large serving bowl or into 8 individual bowls.

4 Bring the syrup to the boil and boil it rapidly until it thickens and reduces. Allow to cool slightly, add the brandy and strain over the pears. Scatter on the toasted nuts, to decorate.

STUFFED PEACHES WITH MASCARPONE CREAM

Mascarpone is a thick, velvety Italian cream cheese, made from cow's milk.

Although it can be used as a thickening agent in savoury recipes, it is often used

in desserts or eaten with a variety of fresh fruit.

INGREDIENTS

*4 large peaches, halved
and stoned (pitted)
40g/1½oz amaretti, crumbled
30ml/2 tbsp ground almonds
45ml/3 tbsp sugar
15ml/1 tbsp cocoa powder
150ml/¼ pint/⅔ cup sweet
white wine
25g/1oz/2 tbsp butter*

*For the Mascarpone Cream
30ml/2 tbsp caster (superfine) sugar
3 egg yolks
15ml/1 tbsp sweet
white wine
225g/8oz/1 cup mascarpone
150ml/¼ pint/⅔ cup
double (heavy) cream*

Serves 4

1 Preheat the oven to 200°C/400°F/ Gas 6. Using a teaspoon, carefully scoop some of the flesh from the cavities in the peaches, to make a reasonable hollow to hold the stuffing. Place the flesh in a bowl, then transfer to a chopping board, Cut the scooped-out flesh into small pieces.

2 In a glass bowl or a jug, mix together the amaretti, ground almonds, sugar, cocoa and peach flesh. Add enough wine to make the mixture into a thick paste.

3 Spread out the halved peaches in a large buttered ovenproof dish and fill them with the stuffing. Place a small cube of butter on each peach half, then add the remaining wine. Bake for 35 minutes.

4 To make the mascarpone cream, beat the sugar and egg yolks until thick and pale. Stir in the wine, then fold in the mascarpone. Whip the double cream to form soft peaks and fold into the mixture. Remove the peaches from the oven and leave to cool. Serve the peaches at room temperature, with the mascarpone.

VARIATION

As a low-fat alternative to mascarpone cream, mix ½ cup ricotta cheese or fromage frais with 1 tbsp light brown sugar. Spoon the cheese mixture into the hollow of each peach half, using a teaspoon, and sprinkle with a little ground star anise or allspice. Grill for 6–8 minutes and serve.

Christmas Baking

*N*uts and spices, dried fruit and mincemeat are all

reminiscent of Christmas, and they are the main ingredients

in the delicious cakes and biscuits in this baking section.

Some recipes, like the Moist and Rich Christmas Cake, need

advance preparation, while others, like the Christmas

Biscuits, are simple enough to make with children.

Gingerbread is essential to Christmas, and there is a recipe

here that can double as pretty tree decorations. There is the

traditional Italian Panettone and Austrian Stollen,

Hogmanay Shortbread and Ginger Florentines.

Finally, there are two appealing recipes with mincemeat – the

all-time favourite – to ensure that everyone finishes

the festive meal feeling satisfied.

Moist and Rich Christmas Cake

This cake can be made 4–6 weeks before Christmas. During this time, pierce it with a

fine needle and spoon over 30–45ml/2–3 tbsp brandy.

INGREDIENTS

225g/8oz/1⅓ cups sultanas (golden raisins)
225g/8oz/1 cup currants
225g/8oz/1⅓ cups raisins
115g/4oz/1 cup stoned (pitted) and
chopped prunes
50g/2oz/¼ cup halved glacé
(candied) cherries
50g/2oz/⅓ cup mixed chopped
(candied) peel
45ml/3 tbsp brandy or sherry
225g/8oz/2 cups plain (all-purpose) flour
pinch of salt
2.5ml/½ tsp ground cinnamon
2.5ml/½ tsp grated nutmeg
15ml/1 tbsp cocoa powder
225g/8oz/1 cup butter
225g/8oz/1 generous cup soft
dark brown sugar
4 large eggs
finely grated rind of 1 orange or lemon
50g/2oz/⅔ cup ground almonds
50g/2oz/½ cup chopped almonds

To Decorate
60ml/4 tbsp apricot jam
450g/1lb almond paste
450g/1lb ready-to-roll fondant icing
225g/8oz ready-made royal icing

Makes 1 cake

1 The day before baking the cake, soak the dried fruit in the brandy or sherry, cover and leave overnight. The next day, grease a 20cm/8in round cake tin and line it with greaseproof paper.

2 Preheat the oven to 160°C/325°F/ Gas 3. Sift together the flour, salt, spices and cocoa powder. Whisk the butter and sugar together until light and fluffy and beat in the eggs gradually. Finally, mix in the orange or lemon rind, the ground and chopped almonds, dried fruits (with any liquid) and the flour mixture.

3 Spoon into the cake tin, level the top and give the cake tin a gentle tap on the work surface to disperse any air bubbles. Bake for 3 hours, or until a fine skewer inserted into the middle comes out clean. Transfer the cake tin to a wire rack and let the cake cool in the tin for an hour. Transfer the cake to the wire rack, but leave the paper on, as it will help to keep the cake moist during storage. When the cake is cold, wrap it in foil and store it in a cool place.

4 Warm, then sieve (strain) the apricot jam to make a glaze. Remove the paper from the cake, place it in the centre of the cake board and brush over the hot apricot glaze. Cover the cake with almond paste and then a layer of fondant icing. Pipe a border around the base of the cake with royal icing. Tie a ribbon around the sides.

5 Roll out any trimmings from the fondant icing and stamp out 12 small holly leaves with a cutter. Make one bell motif with a biscuit mould, dusted first with sifted icing sugar. Roll 36 small balls for the holly berries. Leave the decorations on greaseproof paper to dry for 24 hours. Decorate the cake with the fondant icing leaves, berries and bell, attaching them to the cake with a dab of royal icing. Allow the icing to dry, then cover the cake and pack in an airtight tin until needed.

Light Jewelled Fruit Cake

This cake can be made up to two weeks before eating it. For serving, brush the top

with hot apricot jam and tie a pretty ribbon around the sides.

INGREDIENTS

115g/4oz/½ cup currants
115g/4oz/⅔ cup sultanas (golden raisins)
*225g/8oz/1 cup quartered glacé
(candied) cherries*
*50g/2oz/½ cup finely mixed chopped
(candied) peel*
30ml/2 tbsp rum, brandy or sherry
225g/8oz/1 cup butter
225g/8oz/1 cup caster (superfine) sugar
finely grated rind of 1 orange
finely grated rind of 1 lemon
4 eggs
50g/2oz/½ cup chopped almonds
50g/2oz/⅔ cup ground almonds
225g/8oz/2 cups plain (all-purpose) flour

To Finish
50g/2oz whole blanched almonds

Makes 1 cake

1 The day before you want to bake the cake, soak the currants, sultanas, glacé cherries and the mixed peel in the rum, brandy or sherry. Cover with clear film and leave overnight. The day you bake the cake, grease and line a 20cm/8in round cake tin or an 18cm/7in square cake tin with a double thickness of greaseproof paper.

2 Preheat the oven to 160°C/325°F/Gas 3. In a large bowl, whisk the butter, sugar and orange and lemon rinds together until they are light and fluffy. Beat in the eggs, one at a time.

3 Mix in the chopped almonds, ground almonds, soaked fruits (with their liquid) and the flour, to make a soft dropping consistency. Transfer to the cake tin. Bake for 30 minutes.

4 Gently place the whole almonds in a pattern on top of the cake. Do not press them into the cake or they will sink during cooking. Return the cake to the oven and cook for a further 1½–2 hours, or until the centre is firm to the touch. Let the cake cool in the tin for 30 minutes. Then remove it and cool completely on a wire rack, but leave the paper on; this helps to keep the cake moist while stored.

Spiced Christmas Cake

This light cake mixture is flavoured with spices and fruit. It can be served with

a dusting of icing sugar and decorated with holly leaves.

INGREDIENTS

*225g/8oz/1 cup butter, plus extra
for greasing*
15g/½oz/1 tbsp fresh white breadcrumbs
225g/8oz/1 cup caster (superfine) sugar
50ml/2fl oz/¼ cup water
3 eggs, separated
*225g/8oz/2 cups self-raising
(self-rising) flour*
7.5g/1½ tsp mixed spice
*25g/1oz/2 tbsp chopped
(candied) angelica*
25g/1oz/2 tbsp mixed (candied) peel
*50g/2oz/¼ cup chopped glacé
(candied) cherries*
50g/2oz/½ cup chopped walnuts
icing (confectioner's) sugar, to dust

Makes 1 cake

1 Preheat the oven to 180°C/350°F/ Gas 4. Brush a 20cm/8in x 1.5 litre/ 2½ pint fluted ring mould with melted butter and coat with breadcrumbs,

VARIATION

Instead of angelica, mixed peel and glacé cherries, use a mixture of raisins and currants, if you prefer.

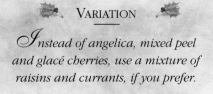

2 Place the butter, sugar and water into a saucepan. Heat gently, stirring occasionally, until melted. Boil for 3 minutes until syrupy, then allow to cool. Place the egg whites in a clean bowl, whisk until stiff. Sift the flour and spice into a bowl, add the angelica, mixed peel, cherries and walnuts and stir well to mix. Add the egg yolks.

3 Pour the cooled mixture into the bowl and beat to form a soft batter. Gradually fold in the egg whites, until the mixture is evenly blended. Pour into the prepared mould and bake for 50–60 minutes or until the cake springs back when pressed in the centre. Turn out and allow to cool on a wire rack. Dust with icing sugar to serve.

PANETTONE

This is a sweet yeast bread that originated in Milan, Italy. It can be served as bread, cake

or even dessert, and is perfect to offer during the festive season.

INGREDIENTS

150ml/¼ pint/⅔ cup lukewarm milk
1 packet easy-blend (rapid-rise)
dried yeast
400g/12–14oz/3–3½ cups plain
(all-purpose) flour
60g/2½oz/⅓ cup granulated (white) sugar
10ml/2 tsp salt
2 eggs
5 egg yolks
175g/6oz/¾ cup unsalted butter, at
room temperature
115g/4oz/¾ cup raisins
grated rind of 1 lemon
75g/3oz/½ cup mixed chopped
(candied) peel

1 Mix the milk and yeast in a warmed mixing bowl and leave to stand for 10 minutes. Sift in 115g/4oz/1 cup of the flour, stir in and cover loosely, and leave it in a warm place for about 30 minutes.

2 Sift over the remaining flour. Make a well in the centre and add the sugar, salt, eggs and egg yolks.

3 Stir the dough mixture until it becomes too stiff, then mix with your hands to obtain a very elastic and sticky dough. Add a little more of the flour, if necessary, blending it in well, to keep the dough as soft as possible.

4 Smear the butter into the dough, then work it in with your hands. When evenly distributed, cover and leave to rise in a warm place until doubled in volume, 3–4 hours.

5 Line the bottom of a 2 litre/3½ pint/ 8 cup charlotte mould or 2 pound coffee can with greaseproof paper, then grease the bottom and sides.

6 Punch down the dough and transfer to a floured surface. Knead in the raisins, lemon rind and citrus peel.

8 Transfer the dough to the mould. Cover with a plastic bag and leave to rise until the dough is well above the top of the container, about 2 hours.

9 Preheat the oven to 200°C/400°F/ Gas 6. Bake for 15 minutes, cover with foil, and lower the heat to 180°C/350°F/ Gas 4. Bake for 30 minutes. Cool in the mould then transfer the cake to a rack.

STOLLEN

Stollen is a fruity yeast bread traditionally served in Austria and Germany at

Christmas-time. It may be served at breakfast with coffee or tea.

INGREDIENTS

150ml/¼ pint/⅔ cup lukewarm milk
40g/1½oz/3 tbsp caster (superfine) sugar
10ml/2 tsp easy-blend (rapid-rise)
dried yeast
350g/12oz/3 cups plain (all-purpose)
flour, plus extra for dusting
1.5ml/¼ tsp salt
100g/4oz/½ cup butter, softened
1 egg, beaten
50g/2oz/⅓ cup seedless raisins
25g/1oz/⅙ cup sultanas (golden raisins)
40g/1½oz/⅓ cup chopped (candied)
orange peel
25g/1oz/½ cup blanched
almonds, chopped
5ml/1 tbsp rum
40g/1½oz/3 tbsp butter, melted
50g/2oz/½ cup icing (confectioner's) sugar

Makes 1 loaf

1 Mix the milk, sugar and yeast and leave in a warm place until it is frothy.

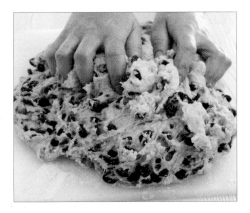

2 Sift the flour and salt and add the yeast mixture. Add the butter and egg and mix to a soft dough. Mix in the dried fruits and nuts with the rum. Knead on a floured board until pliable.

3 Place the dough in a large, greased bowl, cover it with non-stick baking paper and set aside in a warm place for 2 hours, until doubled in size.

4 Turn the dough out on to a floured board and knead it lightly until it is smooth and elastic again. Shape the dough to a rectangle about 25 x 20cm/ 10 x 8in. Fold the dough over along one of the long sides and press the 2 layers together. Cover the loaf and leave it to stand for 20 minutes.

5 Heat the oven to 200°C/400°F/Gas 6. Bake the loaf in the oven for 25–30 minutes, until it is well risen. Allow it to cool slightly on the baking sheet, then brush it with melted butter. Sift the sugar over the top and transfer the loaf to a wire rack to cool. Serve the stollen in thin slices.

De Luxe Mincemeat Tart

The mincemeat can be made up and kept in the refrigerator for up to two weeks.

It can also be used to make individual mince pies.

INGREDIENTS

225g/8oz/2 cups plain (all-purpose) flour
10ml/2 tsp ground cinnamon
50g/2oz/⅔ cup finely ground walnuts
115g/4oz/½ cup butter
50g/2oz/4 tbsp caster (superfine) sugar,
plus extra for dusting
1 egg
2 drops vanilla extract
15ml/1 tbsp cold water

For the Mincemeat
2 dessert apples, peeled, cored and
coarsely grated
225g/8oz/1⅓ cups raisins
115g/4oz ready-to-eat dried
apricots, chopped
115g/4oz ready-to-eat dried figs or
prunes, chopped
225g/8oz green grapes, halved
and seeded
50g/2oz/½ cup chopped almonds
finely grated rind of 1 lemon
30ml/2 tbsp lemon juice
30ml/2 tbsp brandy or port
1.5ml/¼ tsp mixed spice
115g/4oz/generous ½ cup soft light
brown sugar
25g/1oz/2 tbsp butter, melted

Serves 8

1 To make the pastry, put the flour, cinnamon and walnuts in a food processor. Add the butter and process until the mixture resembles fine breadcrumbs. Turn into a bowl and stir in the sugar. Beat the egg with the vanilla essence and water. Gradually stir the egg mixture into the dry ingredients.

2 Gather together to form a soft, pliable dough. Knead briefly on a lightly floured surface until smooth. Then wrap the dough in clear film and chill in the refrigerator for 30 minutes.

3 Mix all of the mincemeat ingredients together in a large bowl.

4 Cut one-third off the pastry and reserve it for the lattice. Roll out the remainder and use it to line a 23cm/ 9in, loose-based flan tin. Make a 5mm/¼in rim around the top edge.

5 With a rolling pin, roll off the excess pastry. Fill the case with mincemeat.

6 Roll out the remaining pastry and cut it into 1cm/½in strips. Arrange the strips in a lattice over the top of the pastry, wet the joins and press them together well. Chill for 30 minutes.

7 Preheat the oven to 190°C/375°F/ Gas 5. Preheat a baking sheet in the oven. Brush the pastry with water and dust with caster sugar. Bake it on the baking sheet for 30–40 minutes. Transfer to a wire rack and cool, then remove the flan tin. Serve warm or cold, with sweetened whipped cream.

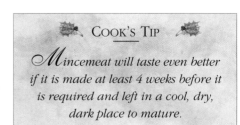

COOK'S TIP

Mincemeat will taste even better if it is made at least 4 weeks before it is required and left in a cool, dry, dark place to mature.

FESTIVE GINGERBREAD

In all its forms, gingerbread has been part of the Christmas tradition for generations.

It is particularly well loved in Germany, from where many present-day baking traditions originate.

INGREDIENTS

30ml/2 tbsp golden (light corn) syrup
15ml/1 tbsp black treacle (molasses)
50g/2oz/¼ cup soft light brown sugar
25g/1oz/2 tbsp butter
175g/6oz/1½ cups plain
(all-purpose) flour
3.5ml/¾ tsp bicarbonate of soda
(baking soda)
2.5ml/½ tsp mixed spice
7.5ml/1½ tsp ground ginger
1 egg yolk

Icing and Decoration
225g/8oz ready-made royal icing
red, yellow and green food colourings
brightly coloured ribbons

Makes 20

1 Preheat the oven to 190°C/375°F/ Gas 5. Line several baking sheets with non-stick baking paper. Place the syrup, treacle, sugar and butter in a saucepan. Heat gently, stirring now and then, until the butter has melted.

2 Sift the flour, bicarbonate of soda, mixed spice and ginger into a bowl. Using a wooden spoon, stir in the trea-cle mixture and the egg yolk and mix to form a soft dough. Remove the dough from the bowl and knead on a lightly floured surface until smooth.

3 Roll out the dough thinly, and using a selection of festive cutters such as stars and Christmas trees, stamp out as many shapes as possible, kneading and re-rolling the dough as necessary. Arrange the shapes, well spaced apart, on the baking sheets. Make a hole in the top of each shape, using a drinking straw, if you wish to use the biscuits as hanging decorations.

4 Bake in the oven for 15–20 minutes or until risen and golden and leave to cool on the baking sheets before transferring to a wire rack using a palette knife.

5 Divide the royal icing into 4 and colour ¼ red, ¼ yellow and ¼ green using the food colourings. Make 4 greaseproof paper piping bags and fill each one with the different coloured icings. Fold down the tops and snip off the points.

6 Pipe lines, dots, and zigzags on the biscuits using the coloured icings. Dry. To hang the biscuits, thread ribbons through the holes made in them.

COOK'S TIP

These brightly decorated gingerbread biscuits are fun to make and can be used as edible Christmas tree decorations.

GINGER FLORENTINES

These colourful, chewy biscuits are delicious served with ice cream, or simply as a teatime treat,

and they make excellent gifts. Store them in an airtight container.

INGREDIENTS

50g/2oz/4 tbsp butter
115g/4oz/8 tbsp caster (superfine) sugar
50g/2oz/¼ cup mixed chopped glacé
(candied) cherries
25g/1oz/2 tbsp chopped (candied)
orange peel
50g/2oz/½ cup flaked almonds
50g/2oz/½ cup chopped walnuts
25g/1oz/1 tbsp chopped glacé
(candied) ginger
30ml/2 tbsp plain (all-purpose) flour
2.5ml/½ tsp ground ginger

To Finish
50g/2oz plain (semisweet) chocolate
50g/2oz white chocolate

Makes 30

1 Preheat the oven to 180C/350°F/ Gas 4. Whisk together the butter and sugar in a mixing bowl until they are light and fluffy. Thoroughly mix in all the remaining ingredients, except for the chocolate.

2 Cut a piece of non-stick baking paper large enough to fit your baking trays. Put 4 small spoonfuls of the mixture on to each tray, spacing them well apart to allow for spreading. Gently flatten the biscuits with the palm of your hand and bake them for 5 minutes.

3 Remove the biscuits from the oven and flatten them with a wet fork, shaping them into neat rounds. Return to the oven for 3–4 minutes, until they are golden brown.

4 Allow the biscuits to cool on the baking trays for 2 minutes, to firm up, and then, using a palette knife, carefully transfer them to a wire rack. When the biscuits are cold and firm, melt the plain and the white chocolate. Spread dark chocolate on the undersides of half the biscuits and spread white chocolate on the undersides of the rest.

Chocolate Kisses

These rich little biscuits look attractive mixed together on a plate and dusted with icing sugar.

Serve them with ice cream or simply as a sweet accompaniment to coffee.

INGREDIENTS

*75g/3oz plain (semisweet) chocolate,
broken into squares
75g/3oz white chocolate, broken
into squares
115g/4oz/½ cup butter
115g/4oz/8 tbsp caster (superfine) sugar
2 eggs
225g/8oz/2 cups plain (all-purpose) flour
icing (confectioner's) sugar, to decorate*

Makes 24

1 Put each pile of chocolate squares into a small bowl and, stirring occasionally, melt them over a pan of hot/not boiling water. Set aside to cool.

2 Whisk together the butter and caster sugar until they are pale and fluffy. Gradually beat in the eggs, one at a time. Then sift in the flour and mix together well.

3 Halve the mixture and divide it between the two bowls of melted chocolate. Mix the chocolate into the dough mixture thoroughly. Knead the doughs until smooth and pliable, wrap them in clear film and set aside to chill them for about 1 hour. Preheat the oven to 190°C/375°F/Gas 5.

4 Shape slightly rounded teaspoonfuls of both doughs roughly into balls. Roll the balls in the palms of your hands to make neater ball shapes. Arrange the balls on greased baking trays and bake them for 10–12 minutes. Dust with sifted icing sugar and then transfer them to a wire rack to cool.

CHRISTMAS BISCUITS

These biscuits are great fun for children to make as presents. Any shape of biscuit cutter can be used.

Store the biscuits in an airtight tin, and for a change, omit the lemon rind and add 25g/1oz/⅓ cup

of ground almonds and a few drops of almond extract.

INGREDIENTS

75g/3oz/6 tbsp butter
50g/2oz/generous ½ cup icing
(confectioner's) sugar
finely grated rind of 1 small lemon
1 egg yolk
175g/6oz/1½ cups plain (all-purpose) flour
pinch of salt

To Decorate
2 egg yolks
red and green edible food colourings

Makes about 12

2 Preheat the oven to 190°C/375°F/ Gas 5. On a lightly floured surface, roll out the dough to 3mm/⅛in thick. Using a 6cm/2½in fluted cutter, stamp out as many biscuits as you can, as close as possible to each other, to get the maximum number of biscuits, with the cutter dipped in flour to prevent it from sticking to the dough.

4 Meanwhile, put each egg yolk into a small cup. Mix red food colouring into one and green food colouring into the other. Using a small, clean paintbrush, carefully paint the colours on to the biscuits. Bake the biscuits for 10–12 minutes, or until they begin to colour around the edges. Let them cool slightly on the baking trays, and then transfer them to a wire rack to cool completely.

1 In a large bowl, beat the butter, sugar and lemon rind together until pale and fluffy. Beat in the egg yolk and then sift in the flour and the salt. Knead together to form a smooth dough. Wrap in clear film and chill for 30 minutes.

3 Transfer the biscuits on to lightly greased baking trays. Mark the tops lightly with a 2.5cm/1in holly leaf cutter and use a 5mm/¼in plain piping nozzle for the berries. Chill on the baking trays for about 10 minutes, until the dough feels firm.

COOK'S TIP

When cooking with young children, things will flow more smoothly if you have all the ingredients prepared before they begin. It is a good idea to provide large aprons for all involved!

ALMOND MINCEMEAT TARTLETS

These delicious little tartlets have a surprise lemon filling and a zesty lemon icing.

Serve them warm with brandy- or rum-flavoured custard.

INGREDIENTS

275g/10oz/2½ cups plain (all-purpose) flour
75g/3oz/generous ¾ cup icing (confectioner's) sugar
5ml/1 tsp ground cinnamon
175g/6oz/¾ cup butter
50g/2oz/⅔ cup ground almonds
1 egg yolk
45ml/3 tbsp milk
450g/1lb jar mincemeat
15ml/1 tbsp brandy or rum

For the Lemon Sponge Filling
115g/4oz/½ cup butter or margarine
115g/4oz/8 tbsp caster (superfine) sugar
175g/6oz/1½ cups self-raising (self-rising) flour
2 large eggs
finely grated rind of 1 large lemon

For the Lemon Icing
115g/4oz/1 generous cup icing (confectioner's) sugar
15ml/1 tbsp lemon juice

Makes 36

1 Sift the flour, icing sugar and cinnamon into a bowl. Rub in the butter. Add the almonds, egg yolk and milk and mix to a dough. Knead until smooth, wrap and chill for 30 minutes.

2 Preheat the oven to 190°C/375°F/Gas 5. Roll out the pastry then cut out 36 rounds to line the tins. Mix the mincemeat with the brandy or rum and put a teaspoonful in each case. Chill.

3 For the lemon sponge filling, whisk the butter or margarine, sugar, flour, eggs and lemon rind together until smooth. Spoon on top of the mincemeat, dividing it evenly, and level the tops. Bake for 20–30 minutes, or until golden brown and springy to the touch. Remove and leave to cool on a wire rack.

4 For the lemon icing, sift the icing sugar into a bowl and mix with the lemon juice to form a smooth, thick, coating consistency. Spoon into a piping bag and drizzle a zigzag pattern over each of the tartlets. Alternatively, if you're very short of time, simply dust the tartlets with sifted icing sugar before serving.

Hogmanay Shortbread

Light, crisp shortbread looks so professional when shaped in a mould,

although you could also shape it by hand.

INGREDIENTS

175g/6oz/¾ cup plain (all-purpose) flour
50g/2oz/¼ cup cornflour (cornstarch)
50g/2oz/¼ cup caster (superfine) sugar
115g/4oz/½ cup unsalted butter

Makes 2 large or 8 individual shortbreads

COOK'S TIP

The secret of successful shortbread baking is to have cool hands when working the butter and sugar together. If you have warm hands or overwork the dough, the fat can become oily.

---

1 Preheat the oven to 160ºC/325ºF/ Gas 3. Lightly flour the mould and line a baking sheet with non-stick baking paper. Sift the flour, cornflour and sugar into a large mixing bowl. Cut the butter into pieces and rub into the flour mixture, using your fingertips or in a food processor. When the mixture binds together, you can knead it into a soft dough, using your hands.

2 Place the dough into the mould and press to fit neatly. Invert the mould on to the baking sheet and tap firmly to release the dough shape. Bake in the preheated oven for about 35–40 minutes or until the shortbread is pale golden in colour.

3 Sprinkle the top of the shortbread with a little caster sugar and set aside to cool on the baking sheet. Wrap the shortbread in cellophane paper and pack in an airtight tin, or place in a box tied with ribbons, to give as a gift.

Stuffings, Sauces and Preserves

*S*tuffings and sauces make up an essential part

of the Christmas fare, but they often require a

lot of preparation time. Because of this, many cooks

forget about them altogether amid the hustle and

bustle of the main events, or decide against them as

an optional extra. It is a good idea to tackle as much

as possible in advance. Many of the recipes here improve

with keeping and most can be stored in the refrigerator or

freezer until they are needed. In the weeks leading up

to Christmas, make the best use of the seasonal produce

available by bottling and preserving it in jars for use

throughout the festive weeks.

APRICOT AND RAISIN STUFFING

INGREDIENTS

40 g/1½oz/3 tbsp butter
1 large onion, sliced
100g/4oz/1 cup dried apricot pieces,
soaked and drained
100g/4oz/⅔ cup seedless raisins
juice and grated rind of 1 orange
1 cooking apple, peeled, cored
and chopped
100g/4oz/2 cups fresh white
breadcrumbs
1.5ml/¼ tsp ground ginger
salt and freshly ground black pepper

Makes about 400g/14oz

1 Heat the butter in a small pan and fry the onion over a moderate heat until it is translucent.

2 Turn the onion into a large mixing bowl and stir in the dried apricots, raisins, orange juice and rind, chopped apple, breadcrumbs and ground ginger.

3 Season with salt and black pepper. Mix well with a wooden spoon, then allow to cool. Use the stuffing to pack the neck end of the bird.

CHESTNUT STUFFING

INGREDIENTS

40g/1½oz/3 tbsp butter
1 large onion, chopped
450g/1lb can unsweetened chestnut purée
50g/2oz/1 cup fresh white breadcrumbs
45ml/3 tbsp orange juice
grated nutmeg
½ tsp caster (superfine) sugar
salt and freshly ground black pepper

Makes about 400g/14oz

1 Heat the butter in a saucepan and fry the onion over a moderate heat for about 3 minutes until it is translucent.

2 Remove the saucepan from the heat and mix the onion with the chestnut purée, breadcrumbs, orange juice, grated nutmeg and sugar.

3 Season with salt and ground black pepper. Allow to cool. Use the stuffing to pack the neck end of the turkey.

CRANBERRY AND RICE STUFFING

INGREDIENTS

225g/8oz/1¼ cups long grain rice, washed
and drained
600ml/1 pint/2½ cups meat or
poultry stock
50g/2oz/4 tbsp butter
1 large onion, chopped
150g/6oz/1 cup cranberries
60ml/4 tbsp orange juice
15ml/1 tbsp chopped parsley
10ml/2 tsp chopped thyme
grated nutmeg
salt and freshly ground black pepper

Makes about 450g/1lb

1 Boil the rice and stock in a small pan. Cover and simmer for 15 minutes. Tip the rice into a bowl and set aside. Heat the butter in a small pan and fry the onion. Add it to the rice.

2 Put the cranberries and orange juice in the cleaned pan and simmer until the fruit is tender. Tip the fruit and any remaining juice into the rice.

3 Add the herbs and season. Allow to cool. Use to pack the turkey neck.

Clockwise from top: Chestnut Stuffing, Cranberry and Rice Stuffing, Apricot and Raisin Stuffing.

Apricot and Orange Stuffing

Ingredients

15g/½oz/1 tbsp butter
1 small onion, finely chopped
115g/4oz/2 cups fresh breadcrumbs
50g/2oz/¼ cup finely chopped
dried apricots
grated rind of ½ orange
1 small egg, beaten
15ml/1 tbsp chopped fresh parsley
salt and freshly ground black pepper

Makes about 400g/14oz

1 Heat the butter in a frying pan and cook the onion gently until tender.

2 Allow to cool slightly, and add the onion to the rest of the ingredients.

3 Mix until thoroughly combined and season with plenty of salt and pepper.

Parsley, Lemon and Thyme Stuffing

Ingredients

115g/4oz/2 cups fresh breadcrumbs
25g/1oz/2 tbsp butter
25g/1 tbsp chopped fresh parsley
2.5ml/½ tsp dried thyme
grated rind of ¼ lemon
1 rasher (strip) streaky (fatty) bacon
1 small egg
salt and freshly ground black pepper

Makes about 400g/14oz

1 In a large bowl, mix the fresh breadcrumbs with the butter. Add the parsley and the thyme with the grated lemon rind.

2 Chop the bacon rasher finely and add to the bowl. Beat the egg and mix all together well.

3 Season generously with salt and ground black pepper and set aside.

Raisin and Nut Stuffing

Ingredients

115g/4oz/2 cups fresh breadcrumbs
50g/2oz/⅓ cup raisins
50g/2oz/½ cup walnuts, almonds,
pistachios or pine nuts
15ml/1 tbsp chopped fresh parsley
5ml/1 tsp chopped mixed herbs
1 small egg, beaten
25g/1oz/2 tbsp melted butter
salt and freshly ground black pepper

Makes about 400g/14oz

1 Mix all the ingredients together thoroughly. Season well with plenty of salt and ground black pepper.

BREAD SAUCE

Smooth and surprisingly delicate, this old-fashioned sauce is traditionally served with roast

chicken, turkey and game birds. If you'd prefer a less strong flavour, reduce the number

of cloves and add a little freshly grated nutmeg instead.

INGREDIENTS

1 small onion
4 cloves
bay leaf
300ml/½ pint/1¼ cup milk
115g/4oz/2 cups fresh white breadcrumbs
15ml/1 tbsp butter
15ml/1 tbsp single (light) cream
salt and freshly ground black pepper

Serves 6

1 Peel the onion and stick the cloves into it. Put it into a saucepan with the bay leaf and pour in the milk.

2 Bring to the boil then remove from the heat and steep for 15–20 minutes. Remove the bay leaf and onion.

3 Return to the heat and stir in the crumbs. Simmer for 4–5 minutes or until thick and creamy.

4 Stir in the butter and cream. Season with salt and pepper and serve.

CRANBERRY SAUCE

This is the sauce for roast turkey, but don't just keep it for festive occasions. The vibrant colour and tart taste

are perfect partners for any white roast meat, and it makes a great addition to a chicken sandwich.

INGREDIENTS

1 orange
225g/8oz/2 cups cranberries
250g/9oz/1¼ cups sugar

Serves 6

1 Pare the rind thinly from the orange, taking care not to remove any white pith. Squeeze the juice.

2 Place the orange rind in a saucepan with the cranberries, sugar and 150ml/¼ pint/⅔ cup water.

3 Bring to the boil, stirring until the sugar has dissolved, then simmer for 10–15 minutes or until the berries burst.

4 Remove the rind. Cool before serving.

Tartare Sauce

This is an authentic tartare sauce to serve with all kinds of fish, but for a simpler version

you could always stir the flavourings into mayonnaise.

INGREDIENTS

2 hard-boiled eggs
1 egg yolk from a large egg
10ml/2 tsp lemon juice
175ml/6fl oz/¾ cup olive oil
5ml/1 tsp chopped capers
5ml/1 tsp chopped gherkins
5ml/1 tsp chopped fresh chives
5ml/1 tsp chopped fresh parsley
salt and white pepper

Serves 6

1 Halve the hard-boiled eggs, remove the yolks and press them through a strainer into a mixing bowl.

2 Using a spatula, blend in the raw yolk and mix thoroughly until smooth. Stir in the lemon juice.

3 Add the oil very slowly, a little at a time, whisking constantly. When it begins to thicken, add the oil more quickly to form a thick emulsion. Use a hand blender (mixer) if you prefer.

4 Finely chop one egg white and stir into the sauce with the capers, gherkins and herbs. Season to taste. Serve as an accompaniment to fried or grilled fish.

Mousseline Sauce

This truly luscious sauce is subtly flavoured, rich and creamy. Serve it as a dip with prepared

artichokes or artichoke hearts, or with fish or poultry goujons.

INGREDIENTS

2 egg yolks
15ml/1 tbsp lemon juice
75g/3oz/6 tbsp softened butter
90ml/6 tbsp double (heavy) cream
salt and freshly ground black pepper
Serves 4

1 To make the sauce, whisk the egg yolks and lemon juice in a bowl placed over a pan of barely simmering water until the consistency is very thick and fluffy.

2 Whisk in the softened butter, adding only a very little at a time; whisk well until it is thoroughly absorbed and the sauce has the consistency of mayonnaise.

3 Using a large balloon whisk, whisk the double cream in a bowl. Continue to whisk the mixture until stiff peaks form.

4 Fold the cream into the egg mixture and adjust the seasoning. You can add a little more lemon juice for extra tang.

Savoury Butters

This selection of eight tiny pots of unusual-flavoured butters can be used as garnishes for meat,

fish and vegetables, as a topping for canapés or as a tasty addition to sauces.

INGREDIENTS

450g/1lb/2 cups unsalted butter
25g/1oz/2 tbsp Stilton
3 anchovy fillets
5ml/1 tsp curry paste
1 garlic clove, crushed
10g/2 tsp finely chopped fresh tarragon
15ml/1 tbsp creamed horseradish
15ml/1 tbsp chopped fresh parsley
5ml/1 tsp grated lime rind
1.5ml/¼ tsp chilli sauce

Makes about 50g/2oz/¼ cup
of each flavour

1 Place the butter in a food processor. Process until light and fluffy. Divide the butter into 8 portions.

2 Crumble the Stilton and mix together with a portion of butter. Pound the anchovies to a paste with a mortar and pestle and mix with the second portion of butter. Stir the curry paste into the third and the crushed garlic into the fourth portion.

3 Stir the tarragon into the fifth portion and the creamed horseradish into the sixth portion. Into the seventh portion add the parsley and the lime rind, and to the last portion add the chilli sauce. Pack each into a sterilized jar with a lid and label. Store in the refrigerator.

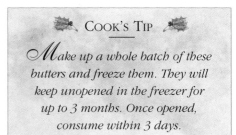

COOK'S TIP

Make up a whole batch of these butters and freeze them. They will keep unopened in the freezer for up to 3 months. Once opened, consume within 3 days.

CHRISTMAS CHUTNEY

This chutney makes the perfect accompaniment to cold meats, pâtés and cheese. It has a sweet

but spicy flavour. The fruits may be changed for quince, greengage or rhubarb.

INGREDIENTS

450g/1lb/9 plums, stoned (pitted)
450g/1lb/6 pears, peeled and cored
225g/8oz/2 cooking apples, peeled and cored
4 celery sticks
450g/1lb onions, sliced
450g/1 lb tomatoes, skinned
115g/4oz/½ cup raisins
15ml/1 tbsp grated fresh root ginger
30ml/2 tbsp pickling spice
850ml/1½ pints/3¾ cups cider vinegar
450g/1lb/2 cups granulated (white) sugar

Makes 1.75kg/4½lb

1 Chop the plums, pears, apples, celery and onions and cut the tomatoes into quarters. Place all these ingredients with the raisins and ginger into a very large saucepan.

2 Place the pickling spice into a square of clean, fine muslin and tie with string to secure. Add to the saucepan of fruit and vegetables with half the vinegar and bring to the boil, stirring. Cook for 2 hours.

3 Meanwhile, sterilize the jars and lids. When all the ingredients are tender, stir in the remaining vinegar and the sugar. Boil until thick, remove the bag of spices and fill each jar with chutney. Cover with a wax paper disc and plastic lid, and label when cold.

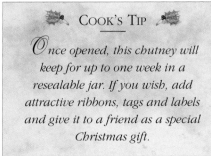

COOK'S TIP

Once opened, this chutney will keep for up to one week in a resealable jar. If you wish, add attractive ribbons, tags and labels and give it to a friend as a special Christmas gift.

Tomato Chutney

This spicy chutney is a delicious accompaniment to a selection of cheeses and biscuits, or with

leftover cold meats. It would also be delicious served with any curried dish.

INGREDIENTS

900g/2lb tomatoes
225g/8oz/1⅓ cups raisins
225g/8oz onions, chopped
225g/8oz/1⅛ cups caster (superfine) sugar
600ml/1 pint/2½ cups malt vinegar

Makes 3 x 450g/1lb jars

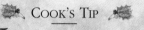

COOK'S TIP

To sterilize the jars, wash them first in hot water then stand upside down to drain. Put the dry jars in the oven at 160°C/325°F/Gas 4 for about 10 minutes.

1 Put the tomatoes in a bowl and pour over boiling water. Leave the tomatoes immersed in the water for 30 seconds, then remove with a slotted spoon and plunge them into cold water. Peel the tomatoes and chop roughly. Put in a preserving pan.

2 Add the raisins, chopped onions and caster sugar to the pan.

3 Pour over the vinegar. Bring the mixture to the boil and let it simmer for 2 hours, uncovered, then transfer the chutney to prepared sterilized jars. Seal with a wax disc and cover with a tightly fitting cellophane top. Store in a cool, dark place. The chutney will keep well, unopened, for up to a year. Once opened, store in the fridge and consume within a week.

Spiced Pickled Pears

These delicious pears are quick and simple to make and are the perfect accompaniment

for cooked ham, strong-flavoured cheeses or cold meat salads.

INGREDIENTS

900g/2lb pears
600ml/1 pint/2½ cups white wine vinegar
225g/8oz/1 cup caster (superfine) sugar
1 cinnamon stick
5 star anise
10 whole cloves

Makes 900g/2lb

1 Use a sharp knife to peel the pears, keeping them whole and leaving the flesh on the stalks. Heat the white wine vinegar and caster sugar together in a saucepan, stirring continuously, until the sugar has melted. Pour over the pears and poach for 15 minutes.

2 Add the cinnamon stick, star anise and cloves and simmer for 10 minutes. Remove the pears and pack tightly into sterilized jars. Simmer the syrup for a further 15 minutes and strain it over the pears. Seal the jars tightly and store in a cool, dark place.

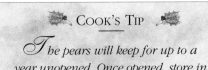

COOK'S TIP

The pears will keep for up to a year unopened. Once opened, store in the refrigerator and eat in one week.

Poached Spiced Plums in Brandy

Bottling spiced fruit is a great way to preserve summer flavours for eating in winter.

Serve these spiced plums as a dessert, with freshly whipped cream, if liked.

INGREDIENTS

600ml/1 pint/2½ cups brandy
rind of 1 lemon, peeled in a long strip
350g/12oz/1⅔ cups caster (superfine) sugar
1 cinnamon stick
900g/2lb fresh plums

Makes 900g/2lb

VARIATION

Other fruits that can be preserved successfully in this way include fresh

1 Put the brandy, sugar and cinnamon stick in a large pan and heat gently to dissolve the sugar. Add the plums and lemon rind. Poach for 15 minutes, or until soft. Remove with a slotted spoon.

2 Reduce the syrup by a third by rapid boiling. Strain it over the plums. Bottle the plums in large sterilized jars. Seal tightly and store for up to 6 months in a cool, dark place.

Rum Butter

No Christmas dinner would be complete without a traditional rich and luscious rum or brandy butter

to accompany the Christmas pudding. This one rounds off the meal perfectly.

INGREDIENTS

225g/8oz/1 cup unsalted butter at room temperature
225g/8oz/1 cup soft light brown sugar
90ml/6 tbsp dark rum or brandy, or to taste

Makes about 450g/1lb

1 Beat the butter and sugar until the mixture is soft, creamy and pale in colour. Gradually add the rum or the brandy, almost drop by drop, beating to incorporate each addition before adding more. If you are too hasty in adding the rum or the brandy, the mixture may begin to curdle.

2 When all the rum has been added, spoon the mixture into a covered container and chill for at least 1 hour.

VARIATION

A variety of liqueurs can be added to the butter and sugar to make delicious alternative accompaniments. Try the recipe with brandy or an orange-flavoured liqueur, or whatever you have to hand.

Index

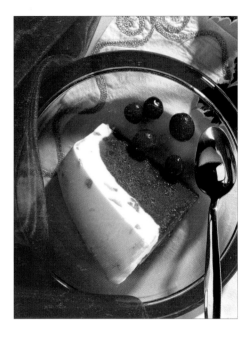